UNDERSTANDING
PSYCHOLOGY

UNDERSTANDING PSYCHOLOGY

Ken Richardson

OPEN UNIVERSITY PRESS
Milton Keynes · Philadelphia

Open University Press
12 Cofferidge Close
Stony Stratford
Milton Keynes MK11 1BY

and
1900 Frost Road, Suite 101
Bristol, PA 19007, USA

First Published 1988
Reprinted 1989

British Library Cataloguing in Publication Data

Richardson, Ken
Understanding psychology.
1. Psychology
I. Title
150

ISBN 0–335–09843–6
ISBN 0–335–09842–8 Pbk

Library of Congress Cataloguing-in-Publication Data

Richardson, Ken.
Understanding psychology / Ken Richardson.
p. cm.
ISBN 0–335–09842–8 (pbk) ISBN 0–335–09843–6
1. Psychology. 2. Psychology—Philosophy. I. Title.
BF121.R45 1988
150'.1–dc19   88–19660 CIP

Typeset by Inforum Ltd., Portsmouth
Printed in Great Britain by The Alden Press, Oxford

Contents

Preface:
The Tower of Babel

Many psychology students I have spoken to complain about the lack of coherence in psychology. By this they usually mean the lack of an overall framework or conceptual scheme, which tends to guide and constrain studies in an advanced science like chemistry or biology, and by which they can make sense of, and relate to each other, the diverse works going on within it. Instead, so the complaint goes, the typical course in psychology consists of a 'theoretical salad', a confusion of fragmentary stands or a conceptual thicket in which it is difficult to see the wood for the trees. This impression all too often leaves students groping for simplifications, diverting into premature specialisation, or simply 'parroting' course material in order to pass exams.

What such students commonly fail to realise is that this is the usual experience of their tutors, too – and, indeed, of academic psychologists, research psychologists and applied psychologists everywhere. Many have complained of this state of affairs in psychology, but few have characterised it quite as well as Karl Pribram (1981, pp. 141–2):

> The fact that the various approaches to psychology have produced a variety of conceptual and experimental frames of psychological inquiry is obvious. Each 'school' of psychology is concerned mainly with its own body of evidence and only dimly aware that alternative schools exist. Such dim awareness can take the form of complete dissociation and denial, of a more or less mild 'put down', or of active conflict. Only rarely . . . is any effort made to examine the relationship of the alternative conceptual-evidential frames to one another. What appears to be lacking is some set of operational definitions that lead from one conceptual domain to another. Only when such definitions become available will there be a non-trivial *modus operandi* for coming to grips with the Tower of Babel that now constitutes scientific psychology.

Statements like this will be of little comfort to the perplexed student. None the less, it is for just such students that the present work is intended. Straight away this implies that some coherence *can* be brought to studies in psychology (and, of course, that this work attempts to bring it); but it does not imply that it is a simple matter. Indeed, 'simple' introductions to psychology need to be treated with suspicion. There are special reasons why psychology is a very complex discipline at the present time and these will be discussed early in the present account. The present work is simply an effort to make that complexity more *understandable*; above all, it seeks to help students come to comprehend psychology.

This effort is motivated by much more than a charitable desire to help students through their exams and to enjoy their courses. The near-sightedness induced by such effects as not being able to see the wood for the trees has very serious consequences for psychology itself. Since criticism is the basis of the growth of all knowledge, it follows that if today's students cannot obtain a critical standpoint with respect to psychology, there will be little growth of knowledge for the benefit of tomorrow's students, and the present state of affairs will persist. It is in order to help students obtain a critical view of psychology, therefore, that the present work is chiefly written. As the quote from Pribram implies, in psychology, there are great works to be done by critical minds!

So what of the scheme adopted? This is fairly easy to summarise. Basically, the vast majority of Western psychological thought is traced to one or other of three 'poles', ideas or sets of presuppositions, namely rationalism, associationism and constructivism. (No apology is made to those who automatically groan in the face of 'isms' in psychology; there are simply no suitable alternatives.) The origins of these ideas, historically, are described, and their rather special 'scientific' status, in relation to society, is explored. Finally, the expression of these ideas in contemporary psychology is illustrated. The advantage of this scheme is that students can relate contemporary psychological ideas to three sets of presuppositions (either singly or as 'admixtures' of them), which can then be properly criticised precisely because of what is *presupposed* (i.e. not empirical fact). Most of modern Western psychology can be understood within this framework.

Of course, it may be argued that the framework is 'old-fashioned', because of its historical dimension; that it is 'ideological' because of its allusions to social forces; or that it is 'selective' because of its analytical breakdown of modern ideas. To the first argument I would say that knowing the history of any discipline is essential for proper understanding of its modern expression. To the second argument I would say that failure to understand the social roots in any science is to fail to understand its 'steering' force. To the third I would simply reply that the scheme proposed accounts for the great majority of modern expressions: no more, no less. In this sense it may be useful to the student as a map for relating and comparing otherwise isolated zones, and thereby giving them a critical purchase on the ground they will cover.

Notice that in relating theories to three fundamental divisions this work is different to most 'introductory' texts in psychology. Like the courses they are designed to serve, these tend either to adopt a particular approach, such as 'developmental', or 'cognitive', or 'information-processing', or alternatively to sample a myriad of areas from, say, 'developmental' through 'learning' to 'social' psychology, to produce the 'theoretical salad' mentioned earlier. The present work does resemble, however, other texts which have attempted to make the subject comprehensible by organising it in fundamental divisions. For instance, many have drawn the line between 'structuralism' and 'functionalism' in psychology. It should become clear in this text why I don't think this division is helpful. The same applies to other proposed divisions such as that between 'positivistic' and 'humanistic' psychology. Closer to the present work is the recent edition of Bower and Hilgard's text *Learning Theories*, in which the authors have used the 'powerful and recurrent' themes of rationalism and empiricism 'to reorganise the chapters of this new edition' (Bower and Hilgard 1981, p. vi).

I believe that these authors are wrong to include constructivism simply as a branch of rationalism, and I treat it here as a separate set of presuppositions. Otherwise, I think this tripartite division is applicable not only to learning theories but to most of the rest of psychology. And so this is the scheme adopted in the present text.

Colleagues in the Centre for Human Development and Learning at the Open University will immediately recognise this scheme as one I have used in my teaching for many years. I am grateful to all of them for criticisms which I hope have yielded some improvements in management and presentation, and also to Margaret van Burken who typed the manuscript and helped in many other ways, and to others like Kevin Moloney who have been encouraging me for years to write such a book.

References

Bower, G. and Hilgard, E.R. (1981) *Theories of Learning* (5th edn.) New York, Appleton.

Pribram, K.H. (1981) The brain as the locus of cognitive controls of action. In G. d'Ydewalle and W. Lens (eds.), *Cognition in Human Motivation and Learning*. Leuven, Leuven University Press and Lawrence Erlbaum Associates.

1

Psychology as Science

The student who aspires to the great insights implied in the term *psychology*, and then stands aghast at the conceptual confusion he or she finds, is a perfect microcosm of the whole history and contemporary state of psychology. Psychology is not an advanced science in the way that physics, chemistry and biology are. In those sciences we have knowledge because a majority of scientists in the field *agree* about what is known: theoretical unity and consensus go together. But psychology lacks such theoretical unity; it therefore lacks consensus about what is and is not 'knowledge' in psychology; and indeed it lacks criteria for judging what might or might not even be acceptable as knowledge in psychology. In other words, the psychologist does not 'know' psychology in the way that the physicist 'knows' physics or the chemist 'knows' chemistry. All that he or she has are personal ideas, opinions or conceptions that may or may not stand up as scientific knowledge as usually accepted by that term. If *psychologists* find it difficult to 'know' psychology, it is hardly surprising that students have the same difficulty.

A number of philosophers have tried to characterise this state of affairs in psychology by comparing it with the advanced sciences, such as physics and chemistry. One popular view of the latter is that these have a clear 'paradigm' (Kuhn 1962; 1971). By this is usually meant an agreed, and therefore dominant, set of presuppositions about the part of nature in question, which guides and governs research and theorising.

> Kuhn's account of the natural sciences emphasises the fact that their scientific status depends essentially on the emergence of a consensus among the community of practitioners as to the authority of a given paradigm . . . [T]his consensus is remarkably absent in the social sciences.
>
> (Gutting 1980, p. 13)

Lakatos (1971), describes psychology, like the other social sciences, as

lacking a coherent 'research programme'; instead it resorts to '*ad hoc* theorising', in which special or particular aspects of the mind are addressed from
several different viewpoints, with little or no attempt to connect them in a
coherent effort. Popper (1971) simply pours scorn on psychology, describing
it as spurious, full of fashions and unbridled dogma.

   Whichever emphasis is most accurate, the lack of a unified approach, or
coherent conceptual scheme (call it what you will), means that scientific
knowledge in psychology is considerably disorganised. Perhaps a useful
analogy is medicine around about the fifteenth century: a discipline in great
social demand, but still dominated by personal or group fashions and weird
practices. Why should psychology be in this state after centuries of investigation? What (if anything) has it been doing wrong? Why are these problems
peculiar to psychology? Understanding psychology means more than simply
'knowing' the disorganised and contradictory 'knowledge' produced by
psychologists; it means actually *recognising* the peculiarity of this state of
affairs. And this, in turn, means understanding psychology as an activity
beset with rather unique difficulties.

Scientific method in psychology

The puzzled student may insist that surely the problem can be solved by a
more energetic and rigorous application of *scientific method* to the questions
they raise. This is a perfectly natural response, but it is not a new one.

   For nearly two centuries, a demand commonly voiced by those concerned
about the backward state of psychology has been that it follow the scientific
methods of the advanced sciences. Only by emulating these methods, so the
argument goes, can it hope to achieve the same discoveries and accumulation
of scientific knowledge. Indeed, great things were expected of an applied,
scientific psychology right from the start of the modern scientific revolution.
Bacon, in his *New Atlantis* (published 1627), wrote seductively of a civilisa-
tion governed by scholars who were trained scientists. Hobbes, in his
Leviathan (1668), went much further in laying down ground rules for the
administration of society based on 'the geometric deduction of the behaviour
of men from the principles of the new science of motion' (cf. Peters 1956, p.
222).

   Even so, for the next two centuries, psychology continued to be dominated by philosophical reasoning and introspectionism. In the nineteenth
century these methods came under increasing attack, most notably by
Augustus Comte, the founder of the school of methodology known as
'positivism' (of which more below). In Britain it was John Stuart Mill who
first translated this positivism into a scientific programme for psychology.
Complaining of the state of psychology as a 'blot on the face of science', he
pleaded for a grand science of society based on the 'laws' of individual

psychology. 'The same processes', wrote Mill in 1829, 'through which the laws of many simpler phenomena have by general acknowledgement been placed beyond dispute must be consciously and deliberately applied to these more difficult enquiries' (quoted by Hearnshaw 1964, p. 5).

Mill's ideas received wide acclaim, and an infant 'scientific' psychology was soon springing up in various parts of the Western world. On the one hand, mental *measurement* was strongly advocated, and Alexander Bain (*The Senses and the Intellect*, 1855; *The Emotions and the Will*, 1859) was the first to follow Mill in this respect. Shortly afterwards Galton was measuring everything from simple reflex times to 'hereditary genius'. On the other hand, an experimental branch developed, culminating in Wilhelm Wundt's *Physiological Psychology* (1873–4). It is now well known how, after the turn of the century, J.B. Watson purged psychology of the last remnants of mental philosophy by rejecting all reference to such unobservable entities as 'mind', 'reason' or 'will' and, in doing so, founded behaviourism.

Behaviourism conformed closely to the positivist philosophy, especially to that development of it known as 'logical positivism'. Logical positivism was the philosophy of Carnap and his followers in Vienna, who insisted that all behaviour should be described and explained in terms of its physically observable manifestations only. 'All sentences of psychology describe physical occurrences, namely the physical behaviours of humans and other animals' (Carnap 1959, p. 165). So, Watson insisted, psychology should approach these physical occurrences just as the other sciences approach (or so he thought) physical occurrences in their own domains.

Behaviourism swept America in the 1930s and found an able propagandist, B.F. Skinner, to carry its message into the post-war era, on both sides of the Atlantic. 'The strategy of physics and biology' must be adhered to, Skinner was still declaring in the 1970s (Skinner 1972, p. 184); our aim must be to establish laws governing the relations between stimuli and responses, which 'expressed in quantitative terms [yield] a comprehensive picture of the organism as a behaving system' (1972, p. 184).

In fact, rigorous experimental scientific methodology was already well established in countless psychology laboratories around the world, and had been for several decades. In the *Introduction to Modern Psychology* (1950, p. ii), Zangwill was quite justified in declaring that 'the foundations of an empirical psychology have been securely laid down during the past sixty years . . . a central biological science of psychology is in process of formation'. Indeed, the modern psychology laboratory is a very impressive-looking place, and anyone involved in experimental psychology will be able to testify to the procedural rigour and statistical sophistication employed in most psychological investigations. As early as 1964, however, Zangwill was expressing his new belief that 'Experimental psychology has produced many facts, a few generalisations, and even an occasional "law". But it has so far failed to produce anything resembling a coherent and generally accepted body of scientific theory' (Zangwill 1964, p. 138).

The same conclusion can be reached today, even in other active fields such as developmental psychology or cognitive psychology, where there have been surges of new investigations, and massive accumulations of fascinating findings. Still we find *ad hoc* theories and little conceptual coherence (see Hearnshaw 1987 for further illustration). The point is, that even a most rigorous emulation of the methods of the natural and physical sciences has not delivered the goods. So it may be instructive to take a closer look at this method with which psychologists are so preoccupied, and examine why it has not been fruitful in the way we would most like, and most need.

The scientific method of science

The foundation of empirical science in the last three centuries has been what is commonly called 'the autonomy of facts'. Science, it is supposed, deals in 'facts' which are revealed to the senses by systematic, objective observation and measurement. The way these facts enter into the whole picture of scientific procedure is illustrated in Figure 1.1. Let us go through this diagram step by step.

1. 'Facts' are revealed by objective observation using standardised (i.e. generally accepted and replicable) techniques and measurements.
2. These facts are assembled into theories. A theory can be thought of as a model of a part of nature – a 'system', with its components described, together with their properties and interrelations. A scientific theory can vary in precision, from a relatively vague set of statements about the system, to a mathematical formula rigorously defining components and relations. ($E = MC^2$ is probably the most famous scientific theory.) The term 'inductive' is sometimes used to describe this aspect of science, i.e. the construing of general principles from specific observables.
3. The *function* of theory is to render the part of nature in question more predictable. This is the whole purpose of the scientific enterprise, whether the 'system' is as small as an atom or as large as the universe. In scientific theory we invariably wish to predict the consequences of a specific perturbation (whether the perturbation arises from nature itself or from a specific human intervention). Accordingly, theory gives rise to predictions. It is the business of experimentation to test theory by testing its predictions.
4. First these predictions have to be translated into the form of a measurable change in one component, resulting from a defined perturbation of one or more others. This is the familiar relation between the 'dependent' and 'independent' variables in experiments. When this translation is com-

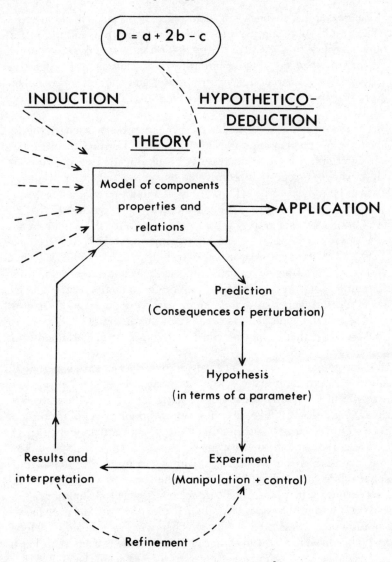

Figure 1.1 The general pattern of scientific research

plete, the prediction becomes a *hypothesis*, and completes the first step in what is known as the hypothetico-deductive aspect of science.

5. A suitably formulated hypothesis is then tested by an appropriately designed experiment, which imposes the perturbation and measures the changes stated within it. (It is at this point, i.e. in the design of experiments, that the ingenuity of the scientist comes to the fore.)

6. The measurable changes – or 'data' – are then analysed and interpreted.
7. The 'results' may confirm the prediction or they may fail to confirm the prediction. If they confirm the prediction they are taken to confirm the theory. If they fail, further interpretation may suggest a fault in the experiment (in the design or procedure) and suggest a refinement for further experimentation (probably the most common result of experiments).
8. If the theory is not confirmed in further experiments, then the theory can be rejected. Further appraisals of the facts, and further theories, need to be entertained. (The term 'research' is obviously a very apt one!)
9. If the theory is repeatedly confirmed by experiments, then at some stage it will be judged to be safe to apply in some practical enterprise.
10. Finally, where 'systems' are being studied which are difficult (or unethical) to manipulate in this direct sense (astronomy and child psychology are obvious examples), a variety of other strategies are used. Thus a 'natural' experiment may arise in which the manipulation has been done for us (for example, an eclipse of the sun, or children reared in different circumstances), and we just have to monitor or compare effects. Alternatively, researchers may simply go on gathering observations in as many and as variable situations as possible. If the theory is valid there are no observations that cannot be contained within it (or explained by it).

This, of course, is rather an idealistic description of what goes on in scientific research, because the whole enterprise is considerably more 'messy' than this. But invariably these sets of 'facts' and testings of theories and predictions are made public in such a way as to allow replication by other workers. Thus scientists, in this rational and objective manner, can select and discard theories and inexorably move closer to 'final truths'. Likewise, anyone claiming to be scientific is claiming to be above prejudice, bias, personal whim or anything else beyond the facts, even when speaking of human nature itself. Science, that is, separates fact from opinion.

So *what* is wrong? This is a marvellously pleasing, rational process, which psychology surely does well to follow. Then why has it failed to deliver the goods? The answer, as already indicated, is that the process is an idealism. Historians of science, who have followed in great detail the fate of theories and experimental testings, have shown that it is not quite as simple as this. It is, indeed, ironic that at the very time psychology has found its scientific feet, the stride it emulates has been critically called into question as an accurate description of science as it is really practised. And the deviation of the reality from the ideal has extremely important implications for the understanding of psychology.

Some of the revelations of the historians of science have to do with the *procedures* of science. The upshot of these is that only rarely have scientists

followed the kind of steps portrayed in Figure 1.1 rigorously; illicit procedures (even among the leaders of the scientific revolution, such as Isaac
Newton) were not uncommon.

Stephen Brush summarised the historian's debunking of numerous alleged
methodological triumphs, and concluded:

> On the basis of the examples I have studied, I suspect that improper
> behaviour is not peculiar to a handful of great scientists but is character-
> istic of a much larger group. Indeed, the burden of proof would seem to
> be on anyone who claims that a majority of scientists habitually use the
> hypothetico-deductive method in the strict sense.
>
> (Brush 1976, p. 81)

Similarly, Feyerabend (1976, pp. 181–2) argues that

> The idea of a method that contains firm, unchanging and absolutely
> binding principles for conducting the business of science gets into
> considerable difficulty when confronted with the results of historical
> research. Indeed, one of the most striking features of recent discussions
> in the history and philosophy of science is the realisation that develop-
> ments . . . occurred either because thinkers *decided* not to be bound by
> certain 'obvious' methodological rules or because they unwittingly
> broke them.

This is not, of course, to argue that the 'methodological rules' should *not* be
adhered to in psychology or anywhere else. The point is, that the fruits of the
advanced sciences have been achieved without such adherence, so that
something *more* than strict adherence to methodology must be required in
psychology.

What this might be is revealed more tellingly when we look more closely at
the belief in the 'autonomy of facts'. The first myth to go was the idea that
scientists readily relinquish theory in the face of countervailing empirical
results. On the contrary, there are numerous illustrations of the way scientists will tenaciously cling to a theory *in spite of* the facts (see Conant 1961,
who covers cases from Copernicus up to the twentieth century, and also
Kessel 1969, and Kuhn 1962). Most revealing, perhaps, is the case of Einstein,
who refused to allow negative experimental facts to shake his confidence in
relativity theory, and who went on to protest that 'it is quite wrong to try
founding a theory on observable magnitudes alone. In reality the very
opposite happens. It is the theory which decides what we can observe'
(quoted by Brush 1976, p. 74).

The lesson of these studies is that no scientific observations or scientific
facts are conceptually neutral; they are already saturated with theory before
the search begins. Michael Polanyi has put this point as follows: 'Every
interpretation of nature, whether scientific, non-scientific, or anti-scientific,

is based on some intuitive conception of the general nature of things . . . The premises of science on which all scientific teaching and research rests are beliefs held by scientists on the general nature of things' (quoted by Kessel 1969, p. 1001). R.G. Collingwood (1940), in his sweeping critique of dogmatic positivism, put it even more succinctly: every scientific statement is the answer to a question; but every question arises from a presupposition.

What this means, as far as the 'autonomy of facts' is concerned, is that we tend to 'see' only those facts that our presuppositions allow us to see. And these, in turn, are assembled into theories that themselves are consistent with the same presuppositions. Clearly, the fruits of scientific theory in the advanced sciences have been due, to a large extent, not to the use of rigorous method, but rather to *presuppositions* about the nature of nature which happened to be conducive to discovery (and, of course – as we shall see later – the freedom actually to impose these presuppositions in criticising and supplanting predecessors). It follows that to understand any science is to understand its presuppositions. This is the conclusion of recent philosophers of science. But where, then, does this leave psychology?

The presuppositions of psychology

We can begin our discussion of what this means for psychology by enlarging slightly on the emergence of facts and their assemblage into theories. This is shown in Figure 1.2.

This diagram indicates how scientific theories arise through cyclical relations at different levels: in particular from presuppositions which themselves help us make sense of ordinary experience. These presuppositions are nothing more than the informal theories, intuitions or preconceptions which we all construct about the things we encounter (plants, animals, motor cars, the weather and so on) in the course of our everyday experiences. We use them in the same way that scientific theories are used, namely to make the world more *predictable*. Even if you have never lifted the bonnet of your car before the occasion when it breaks down, chances are that when you come to do so you will be employing some presupposition or informal theory, however vague, that makes the consequences of your intervention slightly more predictable than a totally 'blind' heaving of pipes and cables.

In other words, scientific theory does not, as a rule, deal with facts which are delivered to the scientist 'raw and pure'; these facts are already saturated with theory (i.e. presuppositions) as soon as they are observed; it is the theory which determines what we can observe.

The history of science is, for the most part, the history of the limitations imposed by those presuppositions, the tensions that result from these limitations and the 'revolutions' which occur when they are surmounted (and new ones are adopted as the basis of new theories). It was 'obvious' to the people

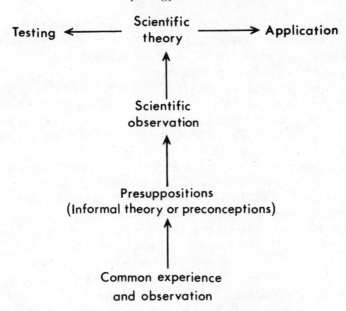

Figure 1.2 The relation between theory and presupposition

of antiquity and of the Middle Ages (and to many people today, who lack the scientific knowledge), that the sun, stars and planets all travel around the earth, as the centre of the universe. For centuries this presupposition, which was both practical, in that it afforded predictability in navigation, agriculture and so on, and ideological, in that it became part of religious authority about 'the order of things', was incorporated into scientific theories of cosmology. When the social order began to change, however, when the ideological order began to lose its grip and increasing criticism broke through, when vastly improved instruments led to countervailing observations, then tensions between presuppositions, scientific theory and facts developed, resulting in the long and painful Copernican revolution in which new presuppositions supplanted the old, giving rise to new theories about origins and movements in the universe. We have to remember that *all* sciences are corrupted by these non-scientific presuppositions to a greater or lesser degree – presuppositions which have their origins in the ordinary experiences and practical problems which scientists share with people in general.

The distinctive feature of psychology as a science is that it generates theories *about people themselves*; and these theories are based on presuppositions which arise from ordinary experience of people. Since we experience people only in a particular social and political reality – i.e. as people *already* organised, in the whole social production process, in a particular way – major presuppositions about human nature (e.g. about human abilities, class and sex differences, child development and so on) naturally arise as direct reflections which tend to explain and legitimise that organisation, and make it seem rational, just and inevitable. Now when psychologists come to do research, gather 'facts' and base their theories on these presuppositions (and are constrained by them in what they can actually 'see') it takes no great imagination to understand how, in doing so, they are incorporating, in a sense, the whole social condition of human nature into those theories. That is, psychologists are constrained by their presuppositions into viewing humanity as it is, or has been, in a particular present or past social order, and have great difficulties in obtaining presuppositions about human nature in any *general* sense or about humanity as it *might be*.

It is not enough to say that psychology is simply more corrupted by social and political presuppositions than other sciences. What we also have to bear in mind is that psychology has frequently been obliged *overtly to embrace and legitimise* those presuppositions, and use its 'scientific' methods and theories to do so. This happens because most of the work psychologists actually do is recruited and paid for by the special institutions of society – employment, education, law, mental health, etc. – which are themselves established to deal with the needs and problems arising from the *maintenance* of a particular social order. Finally, because of changes in the social order, the ideological demands of society frequently change, so that socially originated presuppositions about human nature are also subject to change. These changes may occur quickly (as between, for instance, the generation separating Plato and Aristotle in Ancient Greece, of which more later); more usually they take place over long time-spans. In modern, complex, industrial societies changes both deep and superficial are occurring all the time, and psychologists may 'skip' from one set of presuppositions to another, or switch theoretical emphasis by using different permutations so that a number of conflicting sets of presuppositions will coexist at any one time. Usually, however, these will correspond with different emphases arising from the interplay of complex social forces within these societies. Since there is little coherence among these forces, and indeed much conflict of interest, and therefore of perceptions of human nature, it is scarcely surprising that conceptual incoherence prevails in psychology, in spite of superb methodology.

Understanding psychology

This book is based on the belief that psychology *can* be understood. It can be understood, however, only in the way that we can understand all the sciences, i.e. by understanding its basic presuppositions. Such understanding not only helps us 'keep track' of psychology in its myriad of theoretical expressions; it also puts us in a valuable critical position, because once we understand the assumptions and preconceptions (which are not themselves objective 'facts') underlying a particular theory then we know how to dissect, analyse, assess and criticise it. Only such criticism, as we noted earlier, can expose the weaknesses of theory, encourage the search for more general presuppositions, more detached from historical or contemporary social orders, and lead to the growth and unification of knowledge.

The task of the rest of this book, therefore, is to identify the major presuppositions of psychology and illustrate their manifestations in contemporary theory. Presuppositions at several different levels will be discussed. For the most part, however, these are organised under three headings, corresponding with the different ways humans have been said to 'deal' with their infinitely variable environments. These headings are *rationalism, associationism* and *constructivism*. No apology is made for the use of so many 'isms': they are terms with strong historical roots and are currently apt. Others will be mentioned, however, which either run through or cut across these major divisions.

For instance, there is the presupposition which we will call 'competitive individualism', the belief, stemming mainly from the seventeenth century, that humans, and therefore their minds, exist as encapsulated entities, and that society is purely an 'arrangement' for the furtherance of individualistic interests. Corresponding with this, then, are various presuppositions about how humans *are* drawn into social life (which can be conveniently described as social rationalism, social associationism and social constructivism).

In various places we shall also make reference to presuppositions about the mind, which arise as metaphors of ideological or economic aspects of social life: for instance, the mind as the 'soul' throughout the Middle Ages; the mind as a 'machine', from the seventeenth to twentieth centuries; and, today, the mind as an 'information processor'. Always, however, we shall attempt to show how these presuppositions can be criticised.

But part of understanding psychology is also to do with its potential as a facilitator and liberator for future humankind. The other sciences have had their 'great days'; those of psychology still lie ahead, and, scientifically, these promise to be greater still. We shall talk about this briefly in the final part of the book.

References

Brush, S.G. (1976) Fact and fantasy in the history of science. In M.H. Marx and F.E. Goodson (eds.), *Theories in Contemporary Psychology*. New York, Macmillan.

Carnap, R. (1959) Psychology in physical language. In A.J. Ayer (ed.), *Logical Positivism*. Glencoe, Free Press.

Collingwood, R.G. (1940) *An Essay on Metaphysics*. Oxford, Clarendon Press.

Conant, J.B. (1961) *Science and Common Sense*. New Haven, Yale University Press.

Feyerabend, P.K. (1976) Defence of anarchy. In M.H. Marx and F.E. Goodson (eds.), *Theories in Contemporary Psychology*. New York, Macmillan.

Gutting, G. (ed.) (1980) *Paradigms and Revolutions*. London, Notre Dame.

Hearnshaw, L.S. (1964) *A Short History of British Psychology 1840–1940*. London, Methuen.

Hearnshaw, L.S. (1987) *The Shaping of Modern Psychology*. London, Routledge & Kegan Paul.

Kessel, F.S. (1969) The philosophy of science as proclaimed and science as practiced: identity or dualism? *American Psychologist*, 24, 999–1005.

Kuhn, T. (1962) *The Structure of Scientific Revolutions*. Chicago, University of Chicago Press.

Kuhn, T. (1971) Logic of discovery or psychology of research. In I. Lakatos and A. Musgrave (eds.), *Criticism and the Growth of Knowledge*. London, Cambridge University Press.

Lakatos, I. (1971) Falsification and the methodology of scientific research programmes. In I. Lakatos and A. Musgrave (eds.), *Criticism and the Growth of Knowledge*. London, Cambridge University Press.

Peters, R.S. (1956) *Hobbes*. Harmondsworth, Penguin.

Popper, K. (1971) Normal science and its dangers. In I. Lakatos and A. Musgrave (eds.), *Criticism and the Growth of Knowledge*. London, Cambridge University Press.

Skinner, B.F. (1972) *Beyond Freedom and Dignity*. London, Cape.

Zangwill, O.L. (1950) *An Introduction to Modern Psychology*. London, Methuen.

Zangwill, O.L. (1964) Physiological and experimental psychology. In J. Cohen (ed.), *Readings in Psychology*. London, Allen & Unwin.

2

Rationalism

———

To those who scorn psychology, the surfeit of unusual terms is an easy target.
It is true that there is much gratuitous jargon, and even mysticism, in some
areas of psychology. But equally, any discipline dealing with abstract
concepts requires its fair share of peculiar terms. The natural sciences are full
of 'isms'; and psychology is entitled to them, too. Generally, they are
understandable, so long as they have clear referents, like many terms in
popular use. Most people have little difficulty with fascism, paternalism,
individualism, for instance. Likewise, it is hoped that the 'isms' used in the
next four chapters will be understandable by clarifying what they refer to.
Like all such terms they are used to summarise a multiplicity of meanings
which, none the less, have much in common. As such they are important
terms, and, if we really want to understand psychology in any general sense,
their use is unavoidable.

We start with *rationalism* because it has been one of the most prominent
threads in psychology over the last two thousand years and remains with us
today essentially unchanged. Accordingly, it brings us straight away to face
several important points.

First, it helps us realise the extent to which basic ideas – i.e. the foundations
on which particular contemporary expressions are built – have changed so
little over a very long time indeed.

Second, rationalism brings us to the heart of all psychology, which is to
understand the nature of *knowledge* in humans; how it is achieved; and how it
enters into all our perceptions of the world, and into our behaviour. Again,
this may seem an obscure, or overly philosophical, point, but it is a crucial
one often glossed over in psychology texts and courses. For instance, it
brings us directly into theories and disputes about learning, which has been
described as 'the bedrock of other theories . . . the ultimate fundamental
conceptualisation of human nature' (Gazda and Corsini 1980, p. vii). And
within a broad definition of 'knowing how' and 'knowing that' (as Ryle
defined it), the nature of knowledge underlies almost every other major issue

in psychology, historical and modern.

Finally, rationalism brings us to realise the basis of the difficulties underlying our understanding of knowledge; why it is such a pervasive, persistent
and unsolved problem; and why it produces such disparate and fragmentary
answers. The problem underlying the problem of knowledge is the baffling
one of knowing how knowledge can exist in the face of an infinitely variable,
ever-changing world. This problem requires some pause for thought because
its apparent simplicity is misleading; it is usually glossed over in writings and
courses in psychology; and you would do well to appreciate it fully at the
outset.

The problem is this. Complex animals in general don't live in a constant
world, but instead, experience environments full of objects and events which
are highly variable, forever changing, presenting to the nervous system,
from moment to moment, constellations of stimuli which are only rarely
'familiar', in the usual sense of being direct replications of past experience,
and almost continuously novel. This is true of all complex animals which
move around, forage, hunt, escape from predators, make homes in unfamil-
iar situations and so on, and which are continuously called upon to make
novel responses in these situations. Add to this, in the case of humans, a
whole new stratum of objects and events, in the form of other people with
whom we interact, communicate and co-operate intensively, in a social
world, and you will perhaps begin to see the problem that this poses.

The human situation, in particular, implies a highly complex world of
constant novelty, in which events not only succeed one another rapidly, often
in periods of the order of fractions of a second, but are infinitely more
'fractionated', or broken down, in the sense of a wider variety of combinations of details to attend to. We often have to make 'responses' that are not
only more novel, and infinitely more detailed, than is the case with other
animals, but also ones which 'combine' appropriately with those of, potentially, many other human beings from moment to moment. Consider, for
instance, driving a car, where no situation, from second to second, is quite
like any other, or helping someone move furniture, or playing a game, like
football, or the fact that nearly every linguistic sentence we hear or produce is
one we have never heard or produced before.

William James caught some of this quality of the natural, social environment, when he described the world of the infant as one of 'booming, buzzing
confusion'. What we tend to conclude from this remark is that the 'booming'
and 'buzzing' somehow go away as we grow up, whereas, of course, they are
there all the time; they only become less 'confused' by virtue of the knowledge we manifest in relation to them, and which we use in our perceptions of
them and our motor actions upon them. Conversely, it is sometimes difficult
for us to 'see' or to 'feel' this ever-variable quality of the natural or social
environment, precisely because of our knowledge about it, which makes

what we 'see', and the results of what we do, more predictable. But it is there in great store, none the less, and how we obtain and use this knowledge is at the root of most of our problems in psychology.

An old idea

The essence of rationalism is simply that we are born with the knowledge we have. 'Learning' is simply the process by which we reveal to ourselves the knowledge we already have (but aren't necessarily aware of) by systematic logical deduction or rational discourse: hence the term. The classic examples of this process are the steps taken to reveal mathematical truths, such as principles of geometry, to ourselves and to others. Debate has hinged on issues like whether all, or only certain, domains of our knowledge are inborn; how it develops in childhood; whether experience has any effects at all and, if so, to what extent; and whether we may be born with appetitive and affective 'knowledge' in the same way that we may be born with cognitive knowledge.

The basic principle, however, is a very old one and, like many basic principles in psychology, stems from Ancient Greece. Rationalism is in fact usually traced to Plato, writing around 340 BC (for which reason it is often called 'classical rationalism'), but it is fairly understandable. Many earlier philosophers had drawn attention to the natural 'fluxes' in the experienced world, and speculated on how knowledge could be derived from them. Plato objected to the idea that knowledge could be derived from sense impressions which are forever shifting and changing; true knowledge, he argued, must depend on something more general and stable than these. Instead, he proposed the existence, in the human mind, of the pure 'essences' of these ever-variable objects and events of experience.

For instance, most of the triangles we see are novel, in the sense that few triangles are identical in angulation and side-length. Yet we readily recognise them all as triangles by virtue of recognising something more than what is 'in' each triangle. Likewise, if we are asked to arrange the objects in Figure 2.1 in order of increasing circularity, we can do so because we are in possession of the 'essence' of circularity which is not 'in' each object.

To these essences, Plato gave the name of Ideas or Forms (the terms were used interchangeably). Mentally, these were conceived as transcendental concepts of objects and events, of which those entering into sense-perception are merely distorted exemplars. But these are recognisable, to a degree, as members of their class, by virtue of this concept.

Finally, as already mentioned, these Ideas are innate, or inborn. On this last point Plato presents a famous illustration in which a slave boy, totally without mathematical education, is induced to 'give out' mathematical truths, purely by a process of judicious questioning. Since the boy had not

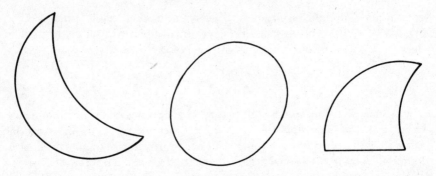

Figure 2.1   Arrange in order of increasing circularity

'learned' these, and did not get them from sense perception, these truths were clearly there all the time, i.e. inborn.

Another important and long-lasting contribution of Plato's psychology was his division of the mind or soul into the cognitive, affective and appetitive domains. The theory of innate ideas obviously applied to the first of these. However, innate determinants of motivation and behaviour were seen to be manifested in the affective and appetitive aspects of the mind also, and these were said to create conflicts in the 'soul' (the cognitive or rational aspect). Here again, Plato used a now famous illustration in which the rational aspect is likened to a charioteer, and the affective and appetitive elements to two horses. The one horse is good (the affective aspect, full of moral courage, honour, etc.), while the other horse is bad (the appetitive aspect); and while the former is easily directed by the charioteer, the bad horse is unruly and subject to sensual passion, so that it must be restrained by the whip. It must be noted that it has been part of rationalist theory, since Plato, that an irrational aspect of the mind (in the form of appetitive urges) has been an integral aspect of rationalist psychology. The rational and irrational are two necessary sides of the same theoretical coin.

The theory of innate ideas passed down the centuries with considerable fluctuation in its popularity, as the typical pendulum swings of psychology favoured one fashion and then another. Its next most significant expression took place in the seventeenth century, when it was considerably embellished and promoted by René Descartes. Like Plato, Descartes objected to the idea that true knowledge came from the mere sensation of objects and events which were changeable and unreliable. True knowledge comes from the application of 'pure thought', which needs to act on the 'essences' of things experienced. 'But as to the essences which are clearly and distinctly conceived, such as that of triangularity or any geometrical figure, I shall easily compel you to acknowledge that the ideas existing in us of these things are not derived from particulars' (quoted in Keeling 1968, p. 181).

Descartes's argument was that no particular sense-impressions exactly exemplify the universals to which they relate, but they are 'distortions' of these, so how could they constitute reliable knowledge? This argument, known as the argument from 'the poverty of the stimulus', greatly impressed Descartes's followers like Spinoza and Leibnitz. When others (as we shall see in the next chapter) were arguing that there is 'nothing in mind but sense impressions', Spinoza replied 'nothing except mind'. It is important to realize that the debate was not merely one taking place on some detached philosophical plane: at stake were crucial implications of the way we learn and think, and therefore of the way that science itself should be practised. Virtually all of the arguments about innate ideas which raged in the seventeenth and eighteenth centuries have fuelled psychological theories and disputes in the twentieth century.

Contemporary rationalism

What we should now do is examine some of the expressions of this set of presuppositions about human nature in contemporary psychology. Note that this exercise will not be exhaustive, but will attempt to give a broad spread of illustrative material – sufficient, at least, to help you identify the same presuppositions in other theories when you come across them, and thus to relate theories to one another. This is one purpose of the exercise. The other is to help you criticise both the general presupposition and its particular expressions in particular theories. A sketch of common criticisms will be offered in the final part of the chapter.

Instinct theories

Advances in biological theory – especially in evolutionary theory – in the nineteenth century gave new impetus to ideas of innate sources of knowledge, and its expression in behaviour. The first effect of Darwin's *Origin of Species* (1859) was the realisation of the co-extensiveness of the human species with the rest of the animal kingdom. Huxley made it clear in his *Man's Place in Nature* (1863), amidst violent religious protest, that humans could no longer be seen to stand alone as a uniquely created order of being. A few years later Darwin himself crystallised the issue for psychology in his *Descent of Man* (1871), and his *Expression of the Emotions in Man and Animals* (1872): 'the mental faculties of man and the lower animals do not differ in kind, though immensely in degree'.

A new branch of psychology, called comparative psychology, quickly sprang up, looking for parallels in the 'intelligence', 'reasoning' or behaviour of animals and humans. And since instincts, or apparently innate tendencies, emotions and behaviour patterns, in animals had long been known and described (and for centuries had been the basis of dog breeding, for instance), it became natural to start looking for instincts in humans. As William James put it in 1890 (p. 194): 'So it has come to pass that the instincts of animals are ransacked to throw light on our own.' Soon psychologists (like James himself) were drawing up lists of human instincts covering everything from hiccupping to making money. This became a very popular pastime among psychologists in the first twenty or thirty years of this century, and psychological theories extended even to broad political tracts extolling the virtues of 'national' instincts, and the vices of 'racial' instincts. For instance, William McDougall, whose book *Introduction to Social Psychology* was based largely on the notion of instincts and became virtually the Bible for psychology students right up to the 1930s (it was reprinted no less than twenty-five times), went on to write books with such titles as *Rudiments of Political Science* (1925) and *Is America Safe for Democracy?* (1921), based on the same notions.

Eventually it came to be realised that the whole business was out of hand, and scepticism, both biological and psychological, set in. This was summarised by Holt (1931, p. 16) when he exclaimed:

> Man is impelled to action, it is said by his instincts. If he goes with his fellows, it is the herd instinct which actuates him; if he fights, it is the instinct of pugnacity; if he defers to another, it is the instinct of self-abasement; if he twiddles his thumbs, it is the thumb-twiddling instinct; if he does not twiddle his thumbs, it is the thumb-not-twiddling instinct. Thus, everything is explained with the facility of magic – word magic.

None the less, instinct theory has survived and flourished in a biologically more respectable framework, at least. This is through the work of ethologists like Tinbergen and Lorenz, painstakingly studying animals in their natural habitats. A large number of characteristic behaviours in fish, birds and mammals have been described in these studies, the stereotyped nature and conditions of 'release' of which have suggested an innate determination.

For example, the greylag goose rolls a loose egg back into the nest with a characteristic backward action of the bill, an action which continues to completion even if the egg meanwhile rolls out of the way. The mandarin drake performs a stereotyped preening of a large ornamental wing feather, and it continues to 'preen' thin air long after the feather has been experimentally cut away. The nest-building of birds represents some of the most complex behavioural sequences in non-human species, and the intricacy sometimes attained is illustrated in the stereotyped stitches used by weaver birds. Other behaviours include the ritualistic mating, threat and other 'displays' reported in numerous species. In each of these a highly specific sign stimulus is said to achieve a 'fixed action pattern' (or FAP), through the mediation of an innate releasing mechanism. Students are advised to read original sources for details of these observations (e.g. Tinbergen 1951; Lorenz 1966; Hinde and Hinde 1975).

But the question is, if such innate 'knowledge' serves other animals in certain circumstances, to what extent are *human* knowledge and behaviour of this type? Clearly, if there are fixed action patterns in humans at all, they are both few and trivial, e.g. simple reflexes like yawning, sneezing and swallowing. However, some ethologists have replied by arguing that, although human action in general is more 'flexible', there are still innate determinants in at least three aspects.

First, in the appetitive or affective domains of human psychology, which give objectives and directions to the cognitive domain and its expression in behaviour. The hunger drive is an obvious example here; others frequently referred to are sex, aggression and the herd instinct, which we have already mentioned.

Second, ethologists have produced observational data which, they claim, is evidence for a wide variety of human facial expressions and gestures acting as sign stimuli. That these expressions, such as the rage grimace or the welcoming eyebrow raising, occur in a wide variety of cultures, with identical interpretation of meaning, points to the conclusion 'that they derive from a common inherited root' (Eibl-Eibesfeldt 1975, p. 455).

Somewhat similar is the idea that humans are susceptible to particular sign stimuli acting on innate releasing mechanisms. The way that faces 'release' the smile of the young infant is an oft-used example. Ethologists have also argued that the affective responses which a person experiences when confronted by a young child, and the caring behaviours which follow, 'are probably released on an innate basis by a number of cues that characterise infants' (Eibl-Eibesfeldt 1975, p. 490).

Finally, is the suggestion by Lorenz and others that innate mechanisms are built 'deep' into our perceptions and thought processes. As Lorenz put it:

> One familiar with the innate modes of reaction of subhuman organisms can readily hypothesise that [innate knowledge in humans] is due to hereditary differentiations of the central nervous system which have become characteristic of the species, producing hereditary dispositions to think in certain forms.
>
> (Lorenz in Evans 1975, p. 183)

Since this idea overlaps with those appearing in other sections, we will discuss it further below.

Personality theories

This has been a most active field of theory production in the twentieth century. Personality is usually defined as a 'stable set of characteristics and tendencies that determine those commonalities and differences in the psychological behaviour (thoughts, feeling and actions) of people that have continuity in time and that may not easily be understood as the sole result of the social and biological pressures of the moment' (Maddi 1980, p. 10). Some psychologists may demur over some of the details of this mouthful, but it would be generally accepted. Because personality theory is very largely about 'inherent attributes' of people, it can clearly be seen to be based on rationalist presuppositions.

Freud is usually depicted as the greatest of the personality theorists, and a discussion of his ideas makes most of the important points. Freud saw the task of the mind, or nervous system, as that of mastering unpredictable, unruly stimuli, impinging both from without (which can be either dealt with or avoided) and from within (which cannot be escaped because they 'maintain an incessant and unavoidable flux of stimulation': Freud 1915, p. 120).

> In Freud's theory this was the task of the mind . . . He developed a series of formulations, principles and spatial metaphors or models (hydrodynamic in nature) to explain the source and fate of 'stimuli' and the means by which the organism accomplished its task of 'mastering' them. These ideas have been modified in significant ways, but still remain at the core of standard psychoanalytic theory.
>
> (Rosenblatt and Thickstien 1977, p. 42)

The internal stimuli arise, in Freud's theory, from the organic needs of the body. These are manifested as the instinctive, or innate, drives – hunger, sex, aggression – which are represented in the 'id', or unconscious mind, and which compel the conscious mind, or 'ego', towards certain goals, according to the external stimuli available. Thus thoughts and actions as well as feelings are expressive of somatic activities and processes. The goals sought ordinarily gratify the instincts according to the 'pleasure principle', but the ego is also affected by the super-ego in which are represented the moral restrictions of the particular social group into which the person has been socialised. Conflicts may break out between these and the basic drives, sometimes leading to neurosis. The goal of psychoanalysis is to seek out these conflicts and help rationalise them.

Whilst Freud's theory explicitly places the innate aspect of behaviour in the representation of basic organic needs, more recent theorists have tried to extend its influence to affect and cognition. Some authors have suggested that these drives, or motivations, are reflected in the whole structuring of trains of thought, (see Rapoport 1952 and Klein 1976, for discussion). And there have been several attempts to establish the core principles of Freudian theory into a 'general psychological' framework, including cognition (e.g. Rosenblatt and Thickstien 1977).

Whilst other personality theorists have been equally convinced about the innateness of the personality core, they have varied in depicting what the core consists of, and also in the way the 'innate' extends to the cognitive and affective as well as the appetitive domains. For instance, Rogers (1963) views the core of personality as a set of general and individual 'potentials'. He is almost completely unspecific about what these are: rather they are assumed to be cognitive, affective and appetitive; and the business of psychology is to understand and help maximise the 'actualisation' of these potentials, under the influence of the environment and personal experience.

Others, such as Eysenck (1967) and Cattell (1965), suggest the existence of stable 'factors' or 'traits' which differentiate broad groups of individuals (e.g. extraverts vs introverts). Eysenck claims that these traits can be related to innately different structures and activities in parts of the nervous system. Of course, theorists vary considerably over the extent to which innate structure is manifested in human personality, as well as the forms it takes. The point is that at some level the presupposition is found in most personality theory.

Language and cognition

One of the most direct links with historical notions of innate ideas among contemporary psychological theories has been expressed in the area of human language. And this in turn has stimulated parallel theories about other aspects of the mind, or about the mind in general.

The 'revolution' in linguistics over the last twenty-five years was instigated mainly by Noam Chomsky, who claimed that previous generations of theorists had failed to appreciate the 'generative' nature of language, i.e. the ability to interpret an infinite variety of verbal stimuli, and to produce an infinite variety of verbal sentences. He also stressed the fact that we develop this ability as children in an extraordinarily short period of time, and on the basis of a limited and imperfect (or 'degenerate') linguistic experience. Chomsky reasoned that it was stretching the bounds of credibility to claim that this came about by any kind of learning (the 'poverty of the stimulus' argument again). Instead, he evoked Descartes's notion of innate ideas and claimed that human children are born with 'innate knowledge' of language – a kind of 'theory' or 'grammar' of the structure, common to all human languages, which allows them to 'crack the code' of the particular language, and to understand and speak it very quickly in the seemingly miraculous way that young children do.

> Suppose that we assign to the mind, as an innate property, the general
> theory of language that we have called 'universal grammar' (language
> universals, both substantive and formal) . . . The theory of universal
> grammar . . . provides a schema to which any particular grammar
> must conform. Suppose, furthermore, that we can make this schema

sufficiently restrictive so that very few possible grammars conforming
to the schema will be consistent with the meagre and degenerate data
actually available to the language learner. His task, then, is to search
among the possible grammars and select one that is not definitely
rejected by the data available to him. What faces the language learner,
under these assumptions, is not the impossible task of inventing a
highly abstract and intricately structured theory on the basis of degenerate data, but rather the much more manageable task of determining
whether these data belong to one or another of a fairly restricted set of
potential languages.

(Chomsky 1968, pp. 75–7)

From this basis of a model for language, Chomsky went on to extend the
model to all the other business of the human mind. As with language, the key
issue was how extremely rich knowledge structures could be derived from
seemingly chaotic and unstructured sensory experience. The physical organs
of the body are not derived from such experience, so why the mental ones?

My own suspicion is that a central part of what we call 'learning' is
actually better understood as the growth of cognitive structures along
an internally directed course under the triggering and partially shaping
effect of the environment . . . Our biological endowment determines
both the scope and limits of physical growth . . . Innate factors permit
the organism to transcend experience, reaching a high level of complexity that does not reflect the limited and degenerate environment . . .
When we turn to the mind and its products, the situation is not
qualitatively different from what we find in the case of the body. Here,
too, we find structures of considerable intricacy, developing quite
uniformly, far transcending the limited environmental factors that
trigger and partially shape their growth . . . We may usefully think of
the language faculty, the number faculty, and others as 'mental organs'
. . . There appears to be no clear demarcation line between physical
organs, perceptual and motor systems, and cognitive faculties in the
respects in question.

(Chomsky 1980, pp. 33–9)

At the same time as Chomsky was developing his theory, a more general
'cognitive revolution' was taking place which leaned heavily on the metaphor
of 'information processing'. The latter grew out of the development of
electronic computers, and attempts were soon being made to simulate human
cognition in these machines (an enterprise now known as artificial intelligence). Gardner (1985) provides a lively account of the confluence of ideas
that emerged, and of their mixed results and prevailing problems. Modern
cognitive theories refer broadly to two components of the mind: the know-

ledge store, and the quasi-mechanical processes which are said to operate on it. In most of these, the machine (and, theoretically, the mind that is being simulated) is provided with certain facts and then programmed to follow certain 'rules', or to process information in a certain way, given certain inputs. By implication – though this is by no means always clear – either the knowledge store or the information processors, or both, are 'built in' or 'hard wired' aspects of the machine and (again theoretically) of the mind. Different theories or models vary considerably on these points.

For instance, working from the standpoint of mental imagery, Roger Shepard has proposed that the ever-changing, variable environment of sense experience can be interpreted only with the aid of innate knowledge, arrived at through natural selection in the course of human evolution. As Gardner (1985, p. 129), describes this idea: 'Whatever the initial focus, such knowledge has been internalised through evolution so that it is now "pre-wired" in individuals and governs how they apprehend objects in space.'

Jerry Fodor (*The Modularity of Mind*, 1983) has proposed a system of information-processing 'modules' in the mind, one for each kind of content, like number, language, vision and music. These are, essentially, 'input systems' which are innate, neurologically distinct, domain-specific and automatic, and carry out all initial analyses on sensory input. Only later are these inputs worked on by central systems, serving 'high-level' cognitive tasks, and which, Fodor believes, will always remain obscure. The idea of such modules or components has become very popular. Gardner (1983) has proposed a theory of 'multiple intelligences': distinct cognitive systems pertaining to different domains of knowledge or competence, whose properties are similar to those described by Fodor for input systems. Sternberg (1984) has proposed a theory of intelligence based, in part, on sets of hypothetical components or information processors. These include 'meta-components', which are used in 'planning, monitoring, and decision-making in task performance'; 'performance components', 'used in the execution of a task'; and 'knowledge-acquisition components', which are 'processes used in learning new things' (Sternberg 1984, p. 282).

Such theorising has also extended from the general to the particular: from general models pertaining to all domains of knowledge and processing, to models restricted to particular domains like reading and mathematics. For instance, Klahr (1984, p. 354) has reflected on cognitive theories of ability in mathematics, asking: 'What is the innate kernel of processes and structures with which the system is endowed?' He finds examples like 'innate cardinality detectors', 'the ability to make ordinal judgements', 'self-teaching mechanisms sensitive to specific information' and 'a numerosity detector'.

A major debate has arisen about the implications in such theories for perception, or the apprehension of the sense data themselves. The debate is between those of the 'ecological school' – mainly followers of J.J. Gibson (e.g. Gibson 1979) – who argue that all the information the organism needs is 'in' the sense data; and the cognitive theorists, who argue that rules and representations *in the mind* are necessary to impose inferences on sense data. As Gardner (1985, p. 317) explains:

> Gibson reflects a belief in the real world as it is, with all the information there, and the organism simply attuned to it; the [cognitivists] reflect a belief in the constructive powers of the mind, with the external world simply a trigger for activities and operations that are largely built into the organism.

This is a debate which raises many fundamental issues, and lays bare the major presuppositions behind the theories. Again, Gardner (1985) provides a lively account.

Constraints on learning

Related to this last group of theories are those which readily admit that experience and learning can account for much of human behaviour, but none the less insist that innate structures exert some quite specific channelling or limiting effect on cognitions, producing differences in learning ability within and between individuals. The upshot of these theories can be summarised as follows:

(a) Humans in general learn some things better than other things.
(b) Some people are good at (i.e. have special aptitudes for) learning some things; other people are good at learning other things.
(c) Some people can learn nearly all things better than other people can.

Property (a) implies that humans, compared with other species, are biologically specially prepared for certain forms of learning (i.e learning in certain domains rather than others). Property (b) suggests that some individuals, compared with other individuals, are specially biologically endowed with 'abilities', 'aptitudes' or 'talents' that make them better at learning particular things. Property (c) is the rationalist theory of 'general learning ability' or 'general intelligence', which is said to vary in a quantitative fashion in any population of humans. We will look at each of these in turn, again to provide illustrations of the theoretical expressions rather than an exhaustive survey.

(a) Preparedness for certain forms of learning

Arguments here are made largely by analogy with the findings from animal research and rely on demonstrating that the animals are predisposed to learn some things better than other things. It is easy to train dogs to do some things but not others; for example, you can teach them to jump through a hoop but not to yawn. Rats very quickly learn to avoid bait that is poisoned and produces nausea, but they learn only very slowly if the bait is not poisoned but associated with foot-shock instead (i.e. in a shock box they are given a mild shock to the feet whenever they try to eat the bait). And to escape from such aversive situations rats will much more readily use some responses, such as running away or jumping out of the shock box, than others, such as pressing a bar or turning a wheel. Similarly, pigeons and bees are good at 'homing', and spiders are good at making webs; the animal illustrations are legion.

Are humans in general similarly prepared to learn some things more easily than others? Some such theories have been proposed. From what we have already discussed it should not be surprising that language has been an obvious candidate. Lenneberg (1967), for instance, has argued that humans are biologically prepared to learn human language in the same way as chaffinches, say, are biologically constrained to learn the chaffinch song rather than that of the blackbird or nightingale. Related to this is the theory of Trevarthen (1983) that the sociability, or 'intersubjectivity', of young infants, which is so much part and parcel of early communication, is innate. Meltzoff and More (1983) have suggested that infants have an innate capacity to imitate the facial gestures of adults and do so very soon after birth. Eimas (e.g. 1982) has presented evidence which has been taken to suggest that infants are born with the capacity to distinguish some of the key sounds of speech – i.e. they have this as innate knowledge.

These are all language, or language-related, areas of knowledge, and in early infancy. It is difficult to find other specific illustrations of lifelong constraints on learning in humans generally. However, many have argued that humans acquire universal mental representations of certain categories because of innate constraints. Thus, it is argued that humans universally categorise the chromatic light spectrum into the four basic colours, red, yellow, blue and green, because of innate (neurophysiological) constraints (see Berlin and Kay 1969; Bornstein 1987). Bornstein (1987) draws a close parallel between vision and audition in these respects, and Eimas, Miller and Jusczyck (1987) express their belief that 'categorisation processes are inherent to human perceptual systems and are functional very early in life without any apparent formal tuition' (p. 162). But these hypotheses, even if valid, refer to what we might call 'low-grade' perceptual constraints; direct parallels in humans, with the sort of constraints apparent in animals, mentioned above, are difficult to find.

(b) Special aptitudes

The idea that some people have special aptitudes is a very common and popular one among psychologists and lay people alike. We often explain special success in a particular field by attributing to the person concerned an inborn talent (a part of the biological make-up of that person, not shared by others). This is particularly so with certain sports and motor skills. But we also apply the idea of special aptitudes to cognitive domains (so that we talk of a 'born teacher' or a 'born salesperson', for instance), and even to particular school subjects (so that we might say of one pupil that 'she has an aptitude for science', or of another that 'he just hasn't got it in him as far as maths is concerned').

This has been an extremely active field of investigation, not only in educational psychology, but also in occupational and industrial psychology, where the aim has been to match the most suitable types of people to particular jobs.

Tyler (1978) has explained how the task of such investigation was to identify an 'ability', thought to be relevant to a particular occupation, of which certain people, it was assumed, possessed a different 'amount'. 'At the outset, it was also assumed that aptitudes were innate rather than learned, that they were based primarily on genetic endowment' (p. 25). Tests were then constructed which were aimed to sample the ability, and thus indicate how much of the aptitude a particular individual had. Tyler, following Ghiselli (1966), then goes on to explain how early high hopes in this movement were dashed by empirical studies revealing very low correlations between test scores and task performance:

> For example, the tests of perceptual speed and accuracy commonly used to select clerical workers have produced correlations with clerical criteria ranging all the way from -0.30, to $+0.49$. The average is about 0.19. With such results, one can hardly talk about clerical aptitude as though it were real and measurable.
>
> (Tyler 1978, p. 93)

The movement has persisted, however, and is, if anything, even stronger today than it was twenty years ago. It has also been revived recently around the topic of 'giftedness' in children (see Meeker 1985 for review).

This area of special aptitudes is one where we find many mixed theories, which involve some biological prestructuring coupled with some associationist or constructivist form of learning. Today the majority of writers hedge considerably on the subject of special aptitudes, though they still range from those who see special aptitudes or abilities as innate, through those who stress some interaction between 'inborn' structures and experience, to those who see aptitudes entirely as a product of experience and circumstance.

(c)   General learning ability or intelligence

Burt (1955) defined intelligence as 'innate, general, cognitive ability'. A succession of psychologists, working in the area of the construction and application of intelligence (IQ) tests, have adopted this definition (e.g. Jensen 1969; 1980; see Humphreys 1985 for review). The ability in question here is usually conceived of as some kind of neurological characteristic conducive to cognitive efficiency. The main point of agreement is that it varies quantitatively within any human population. Thus, analogies with physical 'strength' or 'power', or with 'brightness' and 'dullness' are frequently used. In a critical discussion of this conception Richardson and Bynner (1984) describe it as the 'strength model' of cognition.

There has always been considerable debate about whether there is really a general component at all here, or whether the individual differences in question are best described as different permutations of 'special' abilities or 'components' like numeracy, verbal reasoning, analogical reasoning and so on. And there have been considerable doubts about whether these differences are of anything fundamental, cognitively, anyway. These debates have histories which are too long and complex to go into here (see contributions in Sternberg 1982 for details).

The analogy with simple physical characteristics has had important implications for research strategy in this area. Since the empirical manifestation lies in differences between people, the strategy has been to attempt to show that these differences are genetically determined (this is what so-called 'heritability' estimates are about). Thus has arisen a fierce nature–nurture debate. Again, the details are too complex and voluminous to discuss here; excellent reviews exist (e.g. Wahlstein 1977; Goldberger 1979; see also Richardson 1987), and we shall discuss them further in our general review below. But, again, strong claims have been made which have had enormous impact on psychologists and on educational policy.

Maturation and development

Rationalist presuppositions find frequent and diverse expression in the area of child development. Here, the most usual theoretical formulation is that of 'maturation' – a progressive unfolding of genetically determined structures, both physical and psychological, rather like the budding and blooming of a rose. We have already come across this formulation in the area of language: 'a biological plan unfolds', says Chomsky. But this notion of child development is also very common in other domains. As mentioned earlier, many theories of personality are based on the idea of maturation of innate traits or potentials, cognitive and affective, as well as appetitive.

Actually, there are several ways in which the maturation can be modelled in any given theory, and the particular one most compatible with the theory is usually left implicit. For instance, a model quite common in the nineteenth century was that of 'preformationism'. This followed the claims of the early microscopists to have seen a 'little man' curled up in the head of the spermatozoa, and of the early embryologists who followed the course of development of, for example, chicks in their eggs. This was the idea, then, that development is simply a question of 'growth' of parts and characters that are already there, and are indeed passed on *in toto*, and intact, from parents to offspring.

With the idea of genes, and their particulate nature, becoming accepted after the turn of the century, preformation became replaced to a large extent (but not entirely) by the idea of 'predeterminism'. This model implied that characters were still 'there' in the germ material, only their progressive expression into those of the mature organism was a more complex sequence of transformations and integrations. This idea became dominant in child development, or 'genetic psychology', in the first half of this century and, like preformationism, can still be detected in some theories.

Both of these models impart a very passive role to the environment: so long as it meets certain minimum standards, the characters will 'come out'. Hence, we have heard critics talk about 'the horticultural view of the child', in which the environment is thought of rather in the way we think of manure or fertiliser for plants. A third model – the 'interactive' model – sees a more active role for the environment in shaping the character itself, so that the latter becomes maximally 'adaptive', albeit within certain constraints laid down in the genes. This is perhaps the most common view today among psychologists and is very popular in education. The common use of such expressions as 'providing the best environment for each child to achieve his or her potential' reveals the rationalist ingredient in this view.

Various research studies have attempted to vindicate maturational theories of development. Again, many of these are animal studies, like the famous experiments of Spalding and of Carmichael. The former kept gull chicks in cages, deprived of exercise in flying, until they were well past the normal age of flying. Upon eventual release they were found to be able to fly just like normal gulls. Carmichael added a mild anaesthetic to water containing salamander tadpoles, so these embryos could not swim throughout the period when swimming normally develops. When they were finally placed in fresh water it was observed that they could immediately swim, as if the exercise, or lack of it, was immaterial to development.

This 'deprivation paradigm' has also been used in investigations of motor development in human children. Susan Carey (1981) has reviewed these studies and the kinds of evidence emerging, which 'were taken to support the hypothesis . . . of maturational control of the emergence of motor skills' (p. 3). More recently, more humanely and in the area of cognitive skills, an alternative 'compensatory paradigm' has been employed. Here, children who are assumed to be underdeveloped in cognitive knowledge and skills are given periods of 'environmental enrichment' in order to bring them up to the levels of their potentials. Of course, this entails making assumptions about which environmental 'factors' are most important to this realisation, and therefore of which the child has hitherto been deprived. Large numbers of child development studies have, accordingly, been designed, some involving large 'cohorts' of children studied longitudinally, with the purpose of identifying such supposedly crucial environmental factors. (The best known research in this country is that of the National Child Development Study – see e.g. Fogelman 1983.)

There have been recent attempts to extend Chomsky's views on language development directly to cognitive development. For example, Keil (1981) has argued that development in cognition is governed by 'a priori constraints' on emergent structures and processes. These may be 'special purpose computational systems', 'automatised sub-routines' or a number of other unspecified cognitive elements; whatever they are, the innate constraints are thought to ensure the development of cognitive systems whose 'richness' could not be explained from environmental experience alone. Within this thesis are contained, as we might expect, many of the 'classic' presuppositions of rationalism, to which we will return below.

Finally, there have been many studies aimed explicitly at identifying continuities in child development, again as evidence of maturational processes. What these usually entail, in fact, is the ranking of infants on some measure of (assumed) perceptual or cognitive performance (e.g. habituation to stimuli, or reaction to novel stimuli), and then showing that the ranking prevails to some extent several years later (e.g. Bornstein and Sigman 1986). Since, by the nature of development, the subsequent measures have to be different ones (e.g. standardised 'intelligence' test items) from those used originally, there are many problems of interpretation of such results, although they have been taken as evidence of maturational processes in the cognitive domain. This is further illustration of theory based on rationalist presuppositions.

Review and criticisms

What we have called rationalism, then, is really a set of related presuppositions about the nature of human knowledge and its expression in behaviour. Among these are that knowledge is innate and (in some way) present at conception; that 'learning' is a process of self-realisation of that knowledge through a process of reasoning or 'pure thought'; that human psychological development is analogous to physical development, consisting mainly of a process of growth or maturation; that human psychological differences are also innate; and that the rational content in the cognitive domain is accompanied by irrational urges or drives in the non-cognitive domain. We have illustrated the various ways in which modern scientific theory has built upon and, as it were, both incorporated and legitimated these presuppositions. These are summarised in Figure 2.2.

Several general points need to be remembered about these expressions.

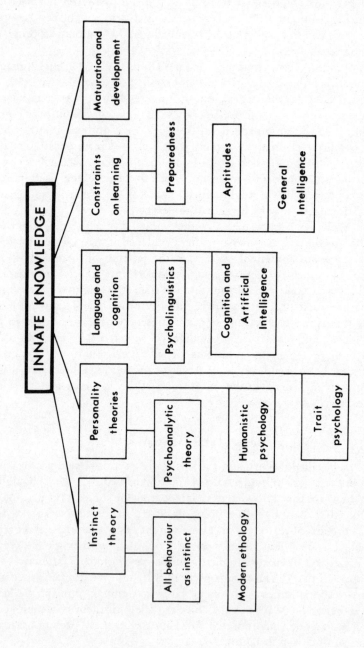

Figure 2.2   Some expressions of rationalism in contemporary theory

First, not all the presuppositions are necessarily or explicitly involved in particular theories. Some stress rationalist principles in the cognitive domain, for instance, whilst ignoring the affective or appetitive domains; other theories stress the appetitive domain; some are concerned chiefly with the maturational process, without being too clear about what it is that matures; and so on. Second, in many, if not most, cases, there has been a 'dressing-up' of the original principles in modern conceptual terms like 'genetic determination', or 'information-processing modules'. And there is frequently expressed moderation concerning the relativity of innate versus empirical knowledge, so that we sometimes hear of experience 'triggering' or partially shaping the expression of the innate kernel, and even of genetic–environment interactions. Finally, as we shall see in subsequent chapters, there are sometimes 'mixed' theories in which rationalism is complemented with a 'dash' of associationism or constructivism.

Underlying these modern emphases and moderations, however, are the same presuppositions, which can be subjected to the same sort of criticisms. The following are the major points of criticism. They do not pretend to be exhaustive; there are almost certainly many others. As mentioned previously, understanding psychological theories is a question of first understanding their fundamental presuppositions. A large number of seemingly disparate psychological theories are in fact united by their common or related presuppositions, so that understanding these should dispel much of the bewilderment students commonly experience in the face of psychological theory. The point of criticism is to help us get beyond this fragmentation, towards more unified theorising in the future. This, at any rate, is the purpose of critical review in this section, as it is in similar sections in other chapters of this book – i.e. a positive impetus to theorising rather than a negative demolition.

The non-scientific origins of presuppositions

It is most important to remember that the presuppositions on which scientific theories are based are not in themselves objective facts or descriptions of reality. They arise as 'informal theories' from everyday experience with nature – in the case of psychology, from experience with other people and their behaviour. But this behaviour may already be determined by the circumstances, the structure of society, for instance, under which people live; all too often the questions about people which psychologists are expected to answer presuppose this structure of society, and also that it is a *consequence* rather than a *cause* of human nature. Hence, there tends to be an interaction between the structure of a society, the political views of psychologists and the theories those psychologists produce.

Much depends on the plausibility of the presuppositions, in two senses. First, repeatedly successful experimental test of a theory may lead to general acceptance among scientists of the validity of the theory, and therefore of the presuppositions on which it is based. Second, the validity of the presuppositions is assessed socially by the success with which they continue to account for social (including economic, industrial and educational) issues. This is a process of 'validation' which can go on independently of the scientific one. Presuppositions about human nature which fly in the face of what is 'obvious' to the popular view will have a very hard time indeed. Many of the most important struggles in science have been precisely about holding out against the 'popular' or 'obvious' view.

As explained in Chapter 1, such has been the complexity of societies in the last two thousand years, and especially modern industrial societies, that no single 'popular' view exists, and therefore no single set of presuppositions. Rather different sets of presuppositions vie for dominance, and achieve it, at different times, often under the influence of social forces dominant at a particular time. The lack of agreement in psychological theorising can to a large extent be attributed to such factors. This is the first criticism to make of rationalist presuppositions, though of course it applies to all sets of psychological presuppositions and, in that sense, is a very general one. The criticisms which follow are much more specific to rationalism.

Theoretical vacuity

Time and again the criticism is made that the conception of 'innateness' has simply become a 'cop-out' from the proper scientific process of theory building. As described in Chapter 1, theories are supposed to specify the components of a system, their properties and the relations between them, so improving our predictability of the world, in the sense of predicting the consequences of certain natural circumstances or of human interventions. To argue that something is 'innate' does none of this, and rationalist scientific theories are, in fact, an improvement on the basic presupposition itself in only a very weak sense. They can indicate how the innate structures 'got there', e.g. by natural selection in the course of evolution. But much more is required if they are to stand as scientific theory; for instance, *what* is innate as a result of *what* selection pressures; *what*, specifically, are the components, with *what* properties and relations, and *what* happens if I do this to that particular component?

To these requirements rationalist psychological theories (at least in the human domain) tend to be silent. Instead, they fall back all too often on *post hoc* rationalisations and special pleadings. *Post hoc* rationalisations usually take the form: 'we have failed to explain this in any other way; surely the causes must, then, be innate'. Special pleadings usually take the form: 'it is obvious that . . . ' or 'clearly . . . ' or 'no one can doubt that . . . '. For example, Keil (1986) uses the expression 'It is difficult to doubt that there are such constraints' (p. 152), when of course we have every right to voice such doubts. We should not be happy with appeals to what is intuitively 'obvious' in science; the whole history of science consists, in many ways, of stubborn progress in overthrowing 'the obvious'. So whenever we see appeals to innate knowledge in psychology we need to demand explicit, scientifically testable, theoretical *details*.

For instance, if you are trying to explain (i.e. provide a theory or useful model of) the categorisation of speech sounds in young infants, it is of little help to say that it is an ability which is 'innate'. This is merely a conjecture – it is neither an explanation nor an observation. All you might be saying is that it is an ability apparently present at birth. Likewise, to say that my concept of 'dog', say, is innate, reveals nothing scientifically. Of course, such conjectures may signal the start of a particular kind of inductive research programme, which would help build a proper theory; but this rarely, if ever, happens.

Imagine you are studying digestion and observe that young infants ingest lots of milk and egest the by-product. What does it reveal to claim that digestion is, therefore, innate? Obviously, a theory requires much more than this. It requires, for instance, a detailed description of the processes themselves (not just the consequences of the processes); an account of the *functions* of the processes; some account of the selection pressures responsible for their evolution; of their expression from genes in the course of early development (showing how this is different from that in *non*-innate characters); and of the environmental conditions of such expression, including the consequences of different environmental perturbations.

Some critics have argued that this 'copping-out' has almost reached the level of deliberate method among the new 'cognitivists', especially those involved in artificial intelligence (see, for example, criticisms among contributions in Costall and Still 1987). The method typically involves drawing flow-charts of information processing in the mind/brain, where information is depicted as passing from one box to another, in each of which processing 'somehow' occurs. Thus, 'each box specifies a function *without* saying how it is to be accomplished (one says in effect: put a little man in there to do the job)' (Dennett 1978, quoted by Palmer 1987, p. 59).

This raises another important point. It is usually assumed that when we conjecture that some knowledge or cognitive process is 'innate', we are putting it in some distinct category. Many authors have exposed the fallacy of such distinct categories as 'innate' and 'learned' (see Chapter 4). What needs to be grasped here, however, are several related points. First is the obvious point that psychological characters don't arise out of thin air. Like all organic characters they are derived from our genes, or at least from the actions and reactions of organic matter, which is itself the expression of our genes. Second, this expression *invariably* requires an environment for it to materialise. Third, the expression will be sensitive to environmental changes or variation, but usually in a non-linear fashion. What this means is that some sub-ranges of an environmental factor will produce little if any change in expression, whereas others might produce huge distortions (Waddington 1975). Finally, there is the notion that this relationship between gene-expression and environmental conditions is itself the consequence of evolutionary selection pressures which (ideally) need to be identified (because the *relationship* varies from character to character).

All that we are saying, then, when we say that some knowledge or cognitive process is innate (as a result, for instance, of all infants apparently having it at birth), is that it has followed a developmental programme, like *all* characters must, but one insensitive to the *range* of environmental variability that those infants have so far experienced. It does *not* mean that the development is somehow insensitive to, or independent of, the environment itself. Thus, the term 'innate' usually is a comment about the conditions under which a character developed, and not about the character itself. Above all, it does not relieve us of the theoretical burden that science demands.

When, for example, Chomsky argues that language and cognitive abilities simply 'grow', like our arms and legs, this is a conjecture and not a scientific theory. It must certainly not be accepted as a conclusion. Of course, such conjectures are important in science; but there is much that needs to be done to turn it into a scientific theory. Resorting to an analogy does not do this, and we immediately need to raise several questions about it. Are the details of the structures and processes, underlying these different characters, the same? Were their evolutionary selection pressures the same? And so on.

A priori structures versus an a priori 'structure-making' device

Note that the issue is not simply about whether or not 'something' is innate, when of course it is biological fact that something is transmitted in genes from parents to offspring. The main question has to do with the extent to which what is transmitted can be, in any sense, *prestructured* knowledge or processes. The constraints argument of Chomsky, Fodor, Keil and others clearly favours considerable prestructuring.

The alternative is some sort of 'structure-making' facility, which reflects the importance of knowledge structures, but leaves the actual construction to be informed from experience in, and action on, the world itself. This is what is implicit in Piaget's theory and is favoured by many others interested in the biological basis of constructivism, as we shall see in Chapter 4.

There are reasons for thinking that innate knowledge structures would, in fact, be a distinct handicap in the human context. Indeed, it has recently been argued that the uniqueness of humans is due precisely to the evolution of adaptability in highly changeable, unpredictable or non-constant environments (Leakey 1981; Mayr 1974; Plotkin and Odling-Smee 1979). The necessity for extreme adaptability is obviously not consistent with a priori constraints, which would soon be 'selected out', whilst an 'all-purpose' system, capable of changing its representational structures frequently and rapidly, would evolve in its place. Scientific practice itself must surely come into this latter category. So there may be a contradiction in the rationalist position, which attributes a 'richness' to innate structures, not obtainable from experience, whereas the variability of experience itself renders fixed structures sooner or later redundant. Rationalists might reply that it depends on the level at which the innate structure is specified (for instance, Chomsky, Keil and others sometimes speak of innate 'rules' or 'constraints' for determining acceptable structures, rather than detailed knowledge structures themselves). But this argument depends, in turn, on the furnishing of testable theoretical details, the paucity of which we have just complained about.

A priori 'richness' versus the 'poverty of the stimulus'

A commonly used underpinning of the constraints approach is that the environment is simply too bland to explain the richness and complexity of human cognitions. As Keil (1981, p. 211) put it: 'The structure of the world hopelessly underdetermines the structures of human mental representation.'

The counter-argument to this point is that psychologists have scarcely examined the structure of the environment, so that its richness, complexity and hidden dynamics may be grossly underestimated. The most consistent theorists behind this point are the 'ecological perception' theorists, particularly J.J. Gibson and E.J. Gibson. According to these theorists the natural and social world is full of information and structure. What humans have to learn are its 'affordances', or 'the possibilities for action that are offered by the objects, events and places that surround us' (Gibson and Spelke 1983, p. 52). More recent application of information theory to relations among stimuli, moreover, has revealed considerable, and previously unsuspected, structure in natural environment that provides the predictability that was previously thought to be absent or impossible (Colwell 1974; Richardson 1983; 1986). This structure may conceivably contain all the necessities for knowledge formation, which have been thought to be the prerogative of 'innate structures' of the mind. In other words, the poverty-of-the-stimulus argument may simply reflect the poverty of our analysis of the natural environment.

Universals and continuities: in the mind or in the world?

We need to point out, briefly, that the evidence evoked in favour of a priori constraints can easily be interpreted in support of opposite arguments. The evidence evoked is usually that implying 'universals' in language and cognition, and 'continuities' in language and cognition.

In language, the point has frequently been made that universals may simply reflect common patterns of human action at a particular time, rather than having a 'final cause' in the structure of language itself. Others have generalised this point to argue that universals in cognitive domains could just as easily reflect extrinsic as intrinsic constraints. Toulmin (1974) uses the example of the neat hexagonal structure of the honeycomb cells in a beehive: surely an example of an a priori structure ('built into' the bees) if ever there was one. But the only constraints operating here may be the purely extrinsic ones of squeezing as many cells as possible into a confined space. Compressing a 'raft' of soap bubbles, for instance, produces an identical effect of cells with a hexagonal structure.

Similarly, with continuities. A continuity in knowledge representation or processes can be interpreted in ways other than a priori constraints: the continuation of extrinsic circumstances that led to that representation in the first place, for instance. Until these can be ruled out it is difficult to gather hard-and-fast evidence in favour of a priori constraints. Certainly, there is no necessity in the argument from universals and continuities to innate structures.

Empirical insufficiency

Presuppositions may become more plausible if repeated tests of theory are successful. The problem is that rationalist theory tends to be so vague and weak, in the human domain, that empirical tests tend to be weak and equivocal. A major strategy has been to attempt to extrapolate more or less directly from animal studies, especially in the area of instincts and fixed action patterns, and the irrational aspects of rationalist theory. But as one ethologist has concluded:

> The actual attempts to attribute FAPs to man have not in fact been very successful. While it is true that, beginning with Darwin's *The Expression of Emotions in Man and Animals* and most recently with the work of Haas and Eibl-Eibesfeldt . . . and Layhausen . . . evidence has accumulated that the expression of emotions is often a FAP, and while there is other evidence for FAPs in man . . . it is also true that FAPish accounts of human behavior in general have been notably lacking in rigor.
>
> For example, there is a considerable amount of loose talk about such and such a characteristic releasing a feeling, an emotion, an aesthetic thrill: i.e. mental events, not behavior patterns . . . They say aggression is innate, but they do not distinguish kinds of aggression . . . and where is the FAP that men use to kill? Where is the species-typical, innate,

releaser? Again, how can such an analysis account for the pervasive influence of learning and culture upon human behavior?

(Cassidy 1979, p. 379)

Further illustrations of empirical weaknesses are to be found in attempts to assess the 'heritability' of characters, as in twin studies. It needs to be stressed above all that such studies are possible only by making some very unlikely assumptions:

(i) that the genes affecting the character act separately but additively, with little flexibility or self-regulation in expression (e.g. that they always act deterministically, against which there is considerable evidence – Waddington 1975);

(ii) that the environment itself can be broken down into a series of 'factors' which similarly have a simple additive 'effect' on the final form of the character;

(iii) that the character has not been subjected to natural selection, so that pairs of identical twins can be considered to be 'special' in sharing all their genes for that trait, whereas pairs of non-identical twins share only half their genes for that trait (in fact, direct comparisons of genetic material suggests that humans share at least 98 per cent of their genes – Washburn 1978);

(iv) that complex psychological characters like human intelligence can be reduced to simple morphological characters like height; and 'measures' of these characters can be thought of, and used in computations, as if they were such linear measures (in fact, most psychometric instruments, like IQ tests, are constructed to go further than this and actually to yield results which 'mimic' simple quantitative characters).

All of these assumptions can be replaced by a number of equally plausible ones, which will then lead to quite different conclusions about the 'heritability' of particular characters (Richardson 1987). Only experimentation, in fact, can help choose between the theoretical alternatives (Kempthorne 1978), but since rationalist theory often tends to be either vacuous or extremely weak, few practicable hypotheses arise (i.e. ones which are both experimentally testable and ethical).

Summary

Rationalism has waxed and waned in psychology for over two thousand years. But it has survived in the late twentieth century to find expression in a vast diversity of psychological theories. These theories are united by sharing rationalist presuppositions. To that extent they can be subjected to the same criticisms. Such criticisms, of course, are not meant to be dismissive of rationalist ideas: but they should serve as a challenge, to those who employ rationalist ideas, to 'firm up' their theories. We have seen, for instance, how 'innateness' of psychological phenomena is often employed as a 'hunch' rather than explicit, testable theory; how extrapolations from other animals to humans, or from simple to complex characters, are unreliable; and how appeals to universals and/or continuities in behaviour are, *on their own*, less than convincing. Also, they should help free theorising from the strait-jacket that rationalism often puts us in. For instance, no one doubts that *something* is transmitted from parents to offspring, biologically. But what it is, and how it 'works', requires the widest possible consideration of factors like the circumstances of human evolution; of 'human ecology'; of the special nature of human social adaptation; of why we need and have these huge brains of ours; and of how these, and the knowledge and cognitions that go on within them, bring us to cope with those circumstances. It is of little, if any, scientific advance simply to argue that something is innate or has a 'biological basis', or to imply that this imposes some necessary constraints on our minds. What has been put in us, biologically, through natural selection, may be creative, inventive and liberating rather than constraining. So there is really much scope for new theory around these questions. This is the point of criticism.

References

Berlin, B. and Kay, P. (1969) *Basic Colour Terms: Their Universality and Evolution.* Berkeley, University of California Press.

Bornstein, M.H. (1987) Perceptual categories in perception and audition. In S. Harnard (ed.), *Categorical Perception: the Groundwork of Cognition.* Cambridge, Cambridge University Press.

Bornstein, M.H. and Sigman, M.D. (1986) Continuity in mental development from infancy. *Child Development*, 57, 251–74.

Burt, C. (1955) The evidence for the concept of intelligence. *British Journal of Educational Psychology*, 25, 158–77.

Carey, S. (1981) Maturational factors in human development. In D. Caplin (ed.), *Biological Study of Mental Processes.* Cambridge, Mass., MIT Press.

Cassidy, J. (1979) Half a century of the concepts of innateness and instinct. *Journal of Comparative Ethology*, 50, 364–86.

Cattell, R.B. (1965) *The Scientific Analysis of Personality.* Baltimore, Penguin.

Chomsky, N. (1968) *Language and Mind.* New York, Harcourt Brace Jovanovich.

Chomsky, N. (1980) *Rules and Representations.* Oxford, Blackwell.

Colwell, R.K. (1974) Predictability, constancy and contingency of periodic phenomena. *Ecology*, 55, 1148–53.

Costall, A. and Still, A. (eds.) (1987) *Cognitive Psychology in Question.* New York, St Martin's Press.

Dennett, D. (1978) *Brainstorms.* Montgomery, Bradford Books.

Eibl-Eibesfeldt, I. (1975) *Ethology.* New York, Holt, Rinehart & Winston.

Eimas, P.D. (1982) Speech perception: a view of the initial state and perceptual mechanisms. In J. Mehler, E.C.T. Walker and M. Garrett (eds.), *Perspectives on Mental Representation*, Hillsdale, New Jersey, Erlbaum.

Eimas, P.D., Miller, J.L. and Jusczyk, P.W. (1987) On infant speech perception and the acquisition of language. In S. Harnard (ed.), *Categorical Perception: the Groundwork of Cognition*. Cambridge, Cambridge University Press.

Evans, R.I. (1975) *Konrad Lorenz: The Man and His Ideas*. New York, Harcourt, Brace, Jovanovich.

Eysenck, H.J. (1967) *The Biological Basis of Personality*. Springfield, Charles C. Thomas.

Fodor, J. (1983) *The Modularity of Mind*. Cambridge, Mass., MIT Press.

Fogelman, K. (ed.) (1983) *Growing up in Great Britain*. London, Macmillan.

Freud, S. (1915) Instincts and their vicissitudes. *Standard Edition*, 117–40. London, Hogarth Press.

Gardner, H. (1983) *Frames of Mind: The Theory of Multiple Intelligence*. New York, Basic Books.

Gardner, H. (1985) *The Mind's New Science*. New York, Basic Books.

Gazda, F. and Corsini, M. (1980) *Theories of Learning*. Itasca, Illinois, Peacock.

Ghiselli, E.E. (1966). *The Validity of Occupational Aptitude Tests*. New York, Wiley.

Gibson, J.J. (1979) *The Ecological Approach in Visual Perception*. Boston, Houghton-Mifflin.

Goldberger, A.A. (1977) *Methods and Models in the I.Q. Debate*. Madison, Wisconsin, Social Science Research Institute, University of Wisconsin.

Hinde, R.A. and Hinde, J.S. (1975) Instinct and Intelligence, Oxford, Oxford University Press.

Holt, E.B. (1931) *Animal Drives and the Learning Process*. New York, Holt.

Humphreys, L.G. (1985) General intelligence. In B.B. Walman (ed.), *Handbook of Intelligence*. New York, Wiley.

James, W. (1890/1950) *The Principles of Psychology*. New York, Dover Publications.

Jensen, A.R. (1969) How much can we boost IQ and scholastic achievement? *Harvard Educational Review*, 39, 1–123.

Jensen, A.R. (1980) *Bias in Mental Testing*, London, Methuen.

Keeling, S.V. (1968) *Descartes* (2nd edn.). Oxford, Oxford University Press.

Keil, F.C. (1981) Constraints on knowledge and cognitive development. *Psychological Review*, 88, 197–227.

Keil, F.C. (1986) On the structure-dependent nature of stages of cognitive development. In I. Levin (ed.), *Stage and Structure: Reopening the Debate*. Norwood, New Jersey, Ablex.

Kempthorne, O. (1978) Logical, epistemological and statistical aspects of nature-nurture data interpretation. *Biometrics*, 34, 1–23.

Klahr, D. (1984) Commentary: an embarrassment of number. In C. Sophian (ed.), *Origins of Cognitive Skills*. Hillsdale, New Jersey, Erlbaum.

Klein, G.S. (1976) *Psychoanalytic Theory: an Exploration of Essentials*, Madison, International University Press.

Leakey, R. (1979) *People of the Lake*. London, Collins.

Leakey, R.E. (1981) *The Making of Mankind*. London, Michael Joseph.

Lenneberg, E. (1967) Biological Foundations of Language, London, Wiley.

Lorenz, K. (1966) *On Aggression*. London, Methuen.

Maddi, S.R. (1980) *Personality Theories.* Chicago, Dorsey Press.

Mayr, E. (1974) Behavior programs and evolutionary strategies. *American Scientist,* 62, 650–9.

Meeker, M. (1985) Toward a psychology of giftedness: a concept in search of measurement. In B.B. Wolman (ed.), *Handbook of Intelligence.* New York, Wiley.

Meltzoff, A.N. and Moore, M.K. (1983) The origins of imitation in infancy: paradigm, phenomenon and theories. In L.P. Lipsitt and K.C. Rovee-Collier (eds.), *Advances in Infancy Research,* Vol. 2. Norwood, New Jersey, Ablex.

Palmer, A. (1987) Cognitivism and computer simulation. In A. Costall and A. Still (eds.), *Cognitive Psychology in Question.* New York, St Martin's Press.

Plotkin, H.C. and Odling-Smee, F.J. (1979) Learning, change and evolution: an enquiry into the teleonomy of learning. *Advances in the Study of Behaviour,* 10, 1–42.

Rapoport, D. (1952) The conceptual models of psychoanalysis. In D. Krech and G.S. Klein (eds.), *Theoretical Models and Personality Theory,* Durham, North Carolina, Duke University Press.

Richardson, K. (1983) Measuring the learning-relevant relations between variables in experience. *Behaviour Research Methods and Instrumentation,* 15, 91–3.

Richardson, K. (1986) Evidence for relational-coding in concept formation. *International Journal of Psychology,* 21, 641–7.

Richardson, K. (1987) Genotype-phenotype relations in models of educational achievement. *British Journal of Educational Psychology,* 57, 1–8.

Richardson, K. and Bynner, J.M. (1984) Intelligence: past and future. In P. Fry (ed.), *Changing Conceptions of Intelligence and Intellectual Functions.* Amsterdam, North Holland.

Rogers, C. (1963) The actualising tendency in relation to 'motives', and to consciousness. In M. Jones (ed.), *Nebraska Symposium on Motivation,* Vol. XI. Lincoln, University of Nebraska Press.

Rosenblatt, A.D. and Thickstien, J.T. (1977) *Modern Psychoanalysis in a General Psychology.* New York, International Universities Press.

Sternberg, R.J. (ed.) (1982) *Handbook of Human Intelligence.* Cambridge, Cambridge University Press.

Sternberg, R.J. (1984) Toward a triarchic theory of intelligence. *The Behavioral and Brain Sciences,* 7, 269–315.

Tinbergen, N. (1951) *The Study of Instinct.* Oxford, Clarendon Press.

Toulmin, S. (1971) Brain and Language: a commentary. *Synthese,* 22, 369–95.

Trevarthen, C. (1983) Interpersonal abilities of infants as generators for transmission of language and culture. In A. Oliveria and M. Zappella (eds.), *The Behaviour of Human Infants.* New York, Plenum Press.

Tyler, L. (1978) *Individuality.* New York, Jossey-Bass.

Waddington, C.H. (1975) *The Evolution of an Evolutionist.* London, Cambridge University Press.

Wahlstein, D. (1979) A critique of the concepts of heritability and heredity in behavioral genetics. In J.R. Royce and L.P. Mos (eds.), *Theoretical Advances in Behaviour Genetics.* Alphen aan den Rijn, Sijtoff and Noordhoff.

Washburn, S.L. (1978) Animal behavior and social anthropology. *Society,* 15, 35–41.

3

Associationism

The modern conceptual foundations of psychology are based on twin pillars which are very ancient. The first of these – rationalism – we have just discussed. The other is *associationism*. What is immediately remarkable about the twin pillars is not simply that they are so ancient, but also that the second was established within a generation of the first; that the author of the second (Aristotle) was the student of the author of the first (Plato); and that these pillars have long been portrayed, to some extent accurately, as being in direct antagonism with each other. In no other discipline could such antagonistic structures coexist for such a long time. And yet, indeed, Aristotle's psychology survives in contemporary theory at least as prominently as that of Plato. This chapter is about tracing the course of that survival through to its modern expressions. As before, some assessment and points of criticism will be offered at the end of the chapter. Some general points about the reasons for the coexistence of these (and other) antagonisms will be left for a later chapter.

At the centre of the antagonism, which still prevails, is the very point of disagreement between Aristotle and his former master: in general the nature of knowledge and its role in human behaviour; in particular the relation between the ever-variable, changeable objects of sense-experience, and the abstract, universalistic ideas that make this chaotic world relatively stable and predictable. Aristotle agreed with Plato, and most of his predecessors (notably Socrates), that these abstract ideas existed. But by declaring that these were innate the Platonists dissolved any connection they might have with the 'real' world of sense experience. Aristotle, however, was an acute and practised observer – as a naturalist cataloguing living things, as an embryologist following the development of chicks in their eggs; and as an anatomist who dissected human bodies. From these activities, i.e. sense experience, he had *acquired* knowledge: knowledge organised and condensed in abstract forms, to be sure, but none the less based on sense experience. The latter could not simply be dismissed as illusion, as the Platonists had insisted.

Thus, Aristotle, as Robinson (1981, p. 80) put it, 'freed himself to use data of experience'. To do this he postulated a special faculty, the faculty of intellect, or reason, that operates on sense-experience to abstract universals of concepts. Although the faculty is innate and imposes form on sense-data, the concepts themselves – representations of natural categories like dogs, cats, triangles, etc. – are not; they are abstracts from sense-experience.

There are two aspects to this fundamental break with the Platonists. The first is concerned with the *method* of realising knowledge. Whereas the Platonists had argued that this consists of a process of 'bringing out' the knowledge that we already have (hence rationalism), Aristotle's version, based on sense experience, is called *empiricism*. This first aspect of the disagreement has created arguments about the pursuit of knowledge, and in particular how science should be practised, that have reverberated down the ages to the present time.

The second aspect has to do with mechanisms: the way that form *is* imposed on sense data to create knowledge. Here Aristotle introduced the notion of mental associations, the registration and storage in the mind of associations occurring in the outside world. The whole universals of Plato could be explained as the abstracted set of features associated in all members of a category. Thus, sense experience with dogs reveals their associated features of four-leggedness, furriness and so on, and these are abstracted by the intellect and placed in memory as the concept of dog. Other associations in the world are captured in memory, too, such as objects and events which are physically similar, which commonly occur together in space or which closely follow one another in time. With sufficient repetition couplets, triplets or longer chains of these associations are formed. They are associated in the sense that evoking one automatically evokes that which usually follows. Thus remembering consists of a mental search for the beginning of such a chain, at which point the rest will automatically follow. Behaviour consists of following through such chains of associations; the response to one stimulus or image presents us with a new image, which evokes a second associated response, and so on. The dinner bell sounds, we move to the table, there we see a chair and move it out, see the seat and sit down, see the spoon and start eating, and so on. Aristotle wrote at some length on 'laws' of association of this sort, most of which are reiterated or echoed in theories of learning and behaviour in the twentieth century.

An important point to make here is that this 'associationism' of Aristotle's was confined to the domains of learning and memory and the empirical source of knowledge. In every other domain of mental phenomena he was a nativist. In the cognitive domain, reason itself is a natural (innate) power in the way that it imposes structure on (abstracts from) sense experience. There are also natural (innate) traits of character (being just, brave, capable or self-centred, and so on) present at birth. And he subscribed to a pleasure principle as the prime mover of behaviour, and thus to a psychology which in the twentieth century became known as behaviourism (of which more below).

It is important to identify this stricture on Aristotle's associationism, because much of the ensuing history of the theory consists of attempts, in turn, to extend it to cover nearly all mental phenomena, and then to return to a more restricted role operating alongside innate, unlearned, irrational phenomena. But as we go through this history, quickly, and then discuss modern expressions of associationism, you should feel certain about one other point: there is nothing complex about the idea; you need not feel that no idea can be so simple, and that therefore you must, somehow, be missing the point. Associationism *is* a simple idea. Things which occur together, or follow each other, in nature will occur together, or follow each other, in the mind. It's as simple as that. Rarely – if ever, in fact – in the history of scientific theory, in any field, has so much been made of such a simple idea.

Through the Dark Ages to the Enlightenment

Either in its empiricist aspect or as associationism, Aristotle's doctrines were passed on in a rich variety of formulations and reinterpretations. Through Augustine, Thomas Aquinas (who, according to Hyman and Walsh, 1973, p. 464, had the task of 'making Aristotle intelligible to the Latins'), Duns Scotus and William of Ockham, knowledge from experience was maintained: but 'from experience' in only a rather passive sense – in the sense of merely 'soaking it up' as it was naturally encountered or observed. From the sixteenth century, methodological empiricism was to change into a much more active pursuit, in a way which gave rise to empirical science itself. As Robinson (1981, p. 203) puts it: 'Renaissance empiricism and experimentalism were based on the motive to control and manipulate nature, to make nature conform and obey, to *change* the world.' The human mind was eventually incorporated under the same programme.

Instead of passively observing, naming and cataloguing, Sir Francis Bacon (*Novum Organum*, 1620) proposed active experimentation – i.e. *changing* nature in small, manageable packets to reveal its underlying laws. In this way, instead of being subjected to nature, 'we should command her in action' (quoted in Johnston 1965, p. 15). In this way *human* nature was to be studied as a branch of nature in general – with the equivalent target of producing more virtuous citizens. With empiricism as the *method* of knowledge production, associationism became increasingly popular as the psychological counterpart.

Various admixtures of conduct based on association and on irrational factors were formulated. Hobbes, for instance, attempted to lay down ground rules for the administration of society based on 'the geometric deduction of the behaviour of men from the principles of the new science of motion' (quoted in Peters 1956, p. 22). In this new world of the seventeenth century, society consisted of individuals driven by personal 'appetites' and 'aversions', satisfied through associations of mechanical sense impressions.

> When a man thinketh on any thing whatsoever, his next thought is not altogether so casual as it seems to be . . . All fancies are motions within us, relics of those made in the sense. And those motions that immediately succeed one another in the sense, continue also together after sense.

> (Hobbes, *Leviathan*, 1651)

Thus in the coming machine age, Hobbes, as Popkin (1966, p. 15) put it, threw in the mind with Descartes's mechanics and saw that 'all mental processes could be understood in terms of physics'.

Locke is usually seen as the founder of 'modern' associationism. The distinctive aspect of Locke's formulation – and those of others who followed him – was the dissolution of the limited role accorded to mental associations by Aristotle. In Locke's scheme, knowledge arises from sensations *acted upon by a faculty of reflection*. The latter is a perceptive faculty which is furnished *with what the senses provide*, and also brings them into touch with the inner state of our emotions or feelings. What the senses furnish, initially, are *simple* ideas: colour, shape, texture, and so on. But by processes of association, these become *complex* ideas, of increasingly higher order – for instance, the idea of an apple from repeated association of 'roundness' and 'redness'. 'But no matter how complex these ideas become, they remain rooted in the soil of experience . . . Locke argues that thinking and perceiving are just different words for the same process' (Robinson 1981, p. 218). In this way, as Anderson and Bower (1973, p. 16) put it: 'The British empiricists extended the domain of associationism from Aristotle's original concern with human memory to encompass all mental phenomena.'

Although we often speak of Locke's view of the mind at birth as a *tabula rasa*, he argued that many aspects of 'character' and 'inclinations of the appetite' are innate (Yolton 1977) and that these played a part in the formation of associations. Thus he recognised that the vividness and durability of mental associations are facilitated when they are augmented by pleasure or pain. And he extended his rules of association into practical spheres like education, where children were to be taught good 'habits' by repetition or drill.

David Hume followed Locke in proposing the formation of complex ideas from simple ideas (*A Treatise on Human Nature*, 1739–40). He emphasised mental associations based on *resemblance* of objects or events; their *contiguity* in time and space; or their frequent *succession* (cause and effect). ' 'Tis plain that in the course of our thinking . . . our imagination runs easily from one idea to any other that *resembles* it, and that this quality alone is to the fancy a sufficient bond and association' (quoted by Laird 1967, p. 43). ' 'Tis evident', he said, 'that the association of ideas operates in so silent and imperceptible a manner, that we are scarcely sensible of it' (ibid.).

Thus Hume's associationism is both strong and pervasive: a kind of reflection in the mind of the relations in the world outside, and extending to all mental phenomena – relations, forms, substances, etc. For Hume, an association 'is a kind of *attraction* which in the mental world will be found to have as extraordinary effects as in the natural', and the laws of association 'are really to *us* the cement of the universe' (quoted by Leahey 1987, p. 112). The corollary of this, in Hume's doctrine, is that all inferences from experience – such as generalised ideas about a category of objects ('all dogs have four legs'), or cause and effect – are consequences of custom or habit, rather than reason. The latter cannot 'know' reality; it can know only internal 'passions', and the rewarding and punishing effects of our conduct. Knowledge so connected with feelings formed *belief*, which is all that distinguishes good judgement from 'the fictions of the imagination' (cf. Robinson 1981).

Thus followed a long debate about the *nature* of these 'connections' and their veracity. Hume was deliberately vague about this. As Laird (1967, p. 40) explains: 'Since Hume was more interested in the conspicuous "effects" of association than in its inexplicable "causes", he tended to pay too little attention to the logical foundations of this theory.' It gave rise, none the less, to considerable popularisation, notably by Hartley and J.S. Mill. As William James later put it: 'These authors traced minutely the presence of association in all the cardinal notions and operations of the mind. The several faculties of the mind were dispossessed; the one principle of association between ideas did all their work' (James 1890/1950, p. 597). James quotes the equally sceptical Priestley, who in 1790 had written:

> Nothing is requisite to make any man whatever he is, but a sentient principle with this single law . . . Not only all our intellectual pleasures and pains but all the phenomena of memory, imagination, volition, reasoning and every other mental affection and operation, are but different modes of cases of the association of ideas.

As we shall see shortly, associationism reached a pinnacle of popularity in the nineteenth century, but by then it had taken on a more practical bent. It is important to consider this bent as a crucial 'bridge' to the development of twentieth-century, and contemporary, behaviourism.

Utilitarianism

Locke, Hume and others had clearly written in support of a particular social and political ideology; and their associationism was a means of underpinning it. By the turn of the nineteenth century, this ideology had become the inspiration of the Radical movement in England, resulting in the Reform Bill of 1832. The philosophical aim of this movement was developed by Jeremy Bentham (*Principles of Morals and Legislation*, 1789) and given the name *utilitarianism*. In reality, the movement took the oft-mentioned role of pleasure and pain in the formation of associations and extended it to society as a whole. 'Nature has placed mankind under the governance of two soveraign masters, *pain* and *pleasure*. It is for them alone to point out what we ought to do as well as to determine what we shall do . . . They govern us in all we do, in all we say, in all we think' (Bentham 1789).

In the context of this pronounced hedonism, Bentham's student, James Mill, followed the popularisers we have just mentioned in reducing all knowledge and operations of the mind to blind associations, but did so in a more explicitly mechanistic portrayal. All knowledge consists of associative links between ideas, by virtue of synchrony or succession of corresponding sensations. Thus, all complex ideas, such as that of a flower or a house, are compounds of associated units (e.g. bricks, boards, nails, etc.). All actions are trains of associated movements. Even speech becomes a train of regularly associated words. As Leahey (1987, p. 143) explains:

> Combined with utilitarian hedonism, the result is a completely mechanistic picture of the mind in which idea follows idea automatically with no room left for voluntary control. The exercise of will is an illusion, Mill maintained. Reasoning is no more than the associative compounding of the ideas contained in syllogisms. Attention . . . is mechanically directed by the principle of utility.

Mill's son, John Stuart Mill, modified these notions to some extent (e.g. *A System of Logic*, 1843), but he still campaigned for associationism. For instance, the younger Mill accepted that human thought and action are not motivated solely by pleasure and pain, for they are capable of self-sacrifice. On the other hand, whereas previous associationists had proposed mental 'links' between ideas, J.S. Mill proposed a 'mental chemistry in which these ideas fused into one'. But like Bentham, he continued to insist that a science of humanity was desirable, and was to be obtained by emulating the natural sciences, chiefly physics. He felt that all social phenomena are simply expressions of individual psychology; and that character could be shaped by a new science of ethology (education). These ideas were, in many respects, a culmination of the 'positivist' view of psychology, proposed by many since Hobbes, but now put more urgently. As such, it provided a crucial bridge to the new expressions in the twentieth century, most of which are still with us today.

Associationism in the twentieth century

In spite of the positivist 'scientific' strand running through this association-ism, it had remained almost totally theoretical, and philosophical, devoid of the sort of empirical, experimental studies common in the natural sciences, which psychologists were being urged to emulate. For this reason, the theorising throughout the period from Hobbes to J.S. Mill is known as 'philosophical associationism'. By the turn of the century, this was to change drastically.

The major impetus behind this change was to be found in the United States of America. It took the form of a preoccupation with *practical* concerns, and therefore with *practical* goals in all spheres of science, including psychology – looking for 'relevance' in social policy, education, child development, etc. An intellectual movement and philosophy known as *pragmatism* came to dominate psychology, with far-reaching influences. A major ingredient in this movement was the setting up of experimental laboratories, emulating that of Wundt in Germany, which many American students had visited. This, as William James noted, brought into psychology an array of young experimentalists, with new objectives. 'There is little of the grand style about these new prism, pendulum and chronograph philosophers. They mean business, not chivalry . . . the experimental method has quite changed the face of science so far as the latter is a record of mere work done' (James 1890/1950, pp. 192–3).

But what ideas were these new, pragmatic experimentalists working *with*? The answer is, mostly associationism. The reason for this, as Anderson and Bower (1973) have pointed out, is that 'it was the most serviceable "learning theory" at hand to meet the needs of educators' (p. 227). The basic, and still very simple, ideas of associationism became almost totally accepted – but associationism with quite a different emphasis from that of the British philosophical associationists. As we have seen, the latter were staunch 'mentalists', in that they attempted to describe and explain mental functions, indeed *all* mental functions, on the basis of mental associations.

What happened in the twentieth century is that, as many commentators have pointed out, psychology 'lost its mind'. Mental functions tended to be forgotten, or deliberately disregarded, in the pursuit of change among, and control of, human beings. Attention switched from the understanding of knowledge and mental functions, to the *control* of behaviour.

Behaviourism

Darwin's theory of evolution had started a major interest in cross-species comparisons, and work on animals was encouraged not only by Darwin's own studies on animal behaviour, and those of Romanes on animal learning, but also by Lloyd Morgan's famous canon of parsimony: 'In no case may we interpret an action as the outcome of the exercise of the higher physical faculty, if it can be interpreted as the outcome of the exercise of one which stands lower in the psychological scale' (Morgan 1894, p. 53).

A colleague of Morgan's in the late 1890s started experimenting with chicks in James's laboratory, and later with cats, dogs and monkeys. His name was Edward L. Thorndike. By watching the progressively more efficient escape strategies of hungry animals from cages (in which tugging a cord released the door), Thorndike and Morgan arrived at the idea of 'trial-and-error learning'. The results of the experiments were published in Thorndike's *Animal Intelligence* in 1898, with all their details of method, measurement, data records, graphs, and so on. Here at last was a realisation of the urge to experiment, to emulate the natural sciences, that had been expressed by the philosophical associationists over the previous two and a half centuries. In the context of the new pragmatism, and evolutionary theory, the fact that the experiments were on animals other than human did not seem to matter.

The movement reached a pinnacle in the assertions of John B. Watson (e.g. Watson 1913), who is usually regarded as the founder of behaviourism in America. Watson's recommendation was that psychologists should ignore mental states altogether; a *scientific* psychology should concern itself only with experimental study or behaviour. 'Psychology as the behaviourist views it is a purely experimental branch of natural science. Its theoretical goal is the prediction and control of behaviour'; moreover, 'The behaviourist . . . recognises no dividing line between man and brute' (Watson 1913, p. 177).

Behaviourism, in its strategy of ignoring mental states, in concentrating instead on the prediction of response outputs by identified stimulus inputs *and* in its recourse to the behaviour of non-human animals as a way of shedding light on our own, swept America over the next twenty or thirty years. Pavlov's work on animals in Russia further strengthened this view, and became incorporated in the general framework. The white laboratory rat became such a focus of psychological research that Tolman (1938, p. 34) could declare: 'I believe that everything important in psychology . . . can be investigated in essence through the continued experimental and theoretical analysis of the determiners of rat behaviour at a choice point in a maze.' And then the general strategy found an able modern propagandist in B.F. Skinner, who still carries the banner of behaviourism in the 1980s.

Note again the crucial point, namely, the side-stepping from the mental states pursued by the philosophical associationists, and the new emphasis on behaviour prediction and control. In this side-stepping, the availability of animals for the purpose of 'real' experimentation seemed a further justification. In this process, though, the 'associations' that had been handed down over the centuries were not entirely forgotten. Rather, they were expressed differently. Instead of being used to explain 'mental states' they were used to explain 'behaviour'. Since these expressions are still prime fodder in the intellectual diet of most psychology students, we need to examine them a little more closely.

Thorndike's connectionism

Thorndike's main experimental results consisted of learning curves, which showed, across repeated trials, the diminishing periods of time required to escape from cages. These curves were related to certain conditions, such as prior food deprivation, and these led to his famous Law of Effect, in which behaviour in a specific situation was postulated to be determined by its satisfying or discomfiting consequences. 'The greater the satisfaction or discomfort, the greater the strengthening or weakening of the bond' (Thorndike 1911, p. 244). This was followed by his Law of Exercise, which simply said that the probability of a response occurring in a given situation increases with the number of times it has occurred in that situation in the past. These laws, Thorndike maintained, emerge, 'clearly in every series of experiments on animal learning and in the entire history of the management of human affairs' (p. 244).

Other, seemingly more complex processes can be reduced to mere secondary consequences of these laws: for instance, abstraction of concepts by similarity among instances; and also selective attention. Even language acquisition in the young could be seen as a process in which some sounds were rewarded in particular situations, while others were not. All of human reasoning could thus be reduced to a kind of habit formation. Although, as Robinson (1981) points out, there is *little* in these laws that had not been postulated by associationists from Aristotle to Bentham – and they had also been clear to animal trainers for centuries – they were here being supported by systematic, experimental findings.

An association in Thorndike's theory was the 'bond' or 'connection' between a response and a situation that was 'stamped in', or eradicated by, the satisfaction or discomfort that resulted from the response. The effective part of the association is a direct bond between the situation (stimulus) and the response. Although he spoke of neurons firing and becoming connected, and of traces of stimuli in the brain, these were undeveloped speculations. Thus, Thorndike went on to present an elaborate S-R (stimulus-response) psychology, which he called connectionism, in which S-R associations, forming networks or hierarchies, strengthen and weaken according to the laws of association, and govern all our behaviour.

Pavlov and classical conditioning

Meanwhile, attacks on 'mentalism' in psychology were also taking place in

Russia, where a school of physiology was already treating behaviour as sets or sequences of reflexes – muscle movements evoked by stimuli. Best known member of this school is I.P. Pavlov, who won the Nobel Prize in 1904 as a result of his studies of digestion. These studies involved collecting and measuring the saliva produced by the salivary glands in dogs. He observed that stimuli other than food sometimes produced salivation, and this led him to study this reflex in some detail as an aspect of behaviour or psychology.

The 'other' stimuli, he realised, were ones which had accompanied the original presentation of food. Thus began one of the most famous series of experiments in psychology, in which a stimulus such as a bell paired with food presentation was, after several trials, found to evoke the salivation by itself. The reflex of salivation thus became known as the conditioned response (CR), and the bell, the conditioned stimulus (CS); whereas the food and reflex alone were called the unconditioned stimulus (UCS) and unconditioned response (UCR) respectively. Pavlov went on to study many aspects of the conditioned reflex, including generalisation to stimuli similar to the CS, and the transfer of the CS-CR pair to a *further* CS, or higher-order conditioning.

What is the nature of Pavlov's associationism, and how does it differ from that of Thorndike? The major difference is that Pavlov saw the conditioning in the association, or learned equivalence, of *stimuli*, rather than the formation of new S-R bonds. For this reason, the process has been called *stimulus substitution* (though it is not really as simple as that, as Bolles, 1975, points out), compared with the *response substitution* of Thorndike and his followers. Pavlov tried to theorise the associations in terms of neural activity, in which 'fields' of activity produced by UCS and CS overlap and establish a neural path. In this way, the two could become more or less equivalent, and the CS could now elicit the reflex originally confined to the UCS. (See Bolles 1975 for discussion.)

The simplicity of his conception notwithstanding, Pavlov was convinced of the generality of its implications for psychology and behaviour. Conditioning was taken to explain all animal and human learning: 'The entire mechanism of thinking consists in the elaboration of elementary associations and in the subsequent formation of chains of association' (quoted by Leahey 1987, p. 285). There was no need to hypothesise mental states of any kind; all learning and behaviour can be explained by the meticulous analysis of environmental stimuli and their associations in relation to bodily reflexes.

Watson's crusade

J.B. Watson became, in effect, the spokesman for behaviourism up to the 1920s. The banishment of the mind from psychology became his aim; and it was very largely achieved. He even found Thorndike's use of terms like 'satisfying', 'discomfort' and 'mental bond' rather too mentalistic, and preferred the radical 'objectivity' of Pavlov. Everything mental, he argued could be conceived as stimuli and responses: for instance, emotions and other feelings are stimuli arising from within the body; all aspects of conscious awareness are kinaesthetic stimuli arising from the muscles of the body; even thought is 'inner speech', consisting of minute movements in the larynx, or voice-box.

Watson's associationism was similar to Thorndike's in that he postulated that when a stimulus and a response occur together the association is strengthened. But Watson eschewed the Law of Effect (and its mentalistic connotations), and instead emphasised the role of frequency or exercise. And he tried to express the associations in terms of neural activity: specifically, he argued that activities are created by stimulus and response in different parts of the brain, and that when these occur together neural pathways between them are used and strengthen with repetition. He argued that these connections are not formed or unformed in the process, rather they are already there as part of our organic constitution; experience simply lowers the threshold of activity along them. By such means he offered an explanation of classical condition-ing different from that of Pavlov's: because the CS and UR occur together the congenital connection between *them* (as well as between the UCS and UR) opens up and strengthens with repetition. As Bolles (1975) points out, this involves the strange assumption that there must be latent connections in the brain between all possible stimuli and all possible responses. This is what distinguishes Watson's associationism as a process of *incrementation*, rather than making or breaking of connections.

Skinner's radical behaviourism

By insisting on behaviour as the proper subject of psychology, B.F. Skinner has carried the banner of behaviourism through to the 1980s. 'Behaviour itself is its fundamental subject matter; behaviour is not an indirect means of studying something else, such as cognition or mind or brain' (Catania 1984, p. 473). It is not that the latter do not exist – only that they are not relevant to prediction and control of behaviour, and thus time-wasting. Most of the heated debate which Skinner's theory has generated is concerned with his particular 'scientific strategy' of ignoring inner states and concentrating on the analysis and description of observable and predictable aspects of be-haviour. We will not delve into these arguments too much here, partly because they will echo points already made, and partly because the literature created by them is voluminous enough already. (Interested students are particularly directed to the publication of 'Canonical Papers of B.F. Skinner', together with peer commentaries, in a special issue of the journal, *The Behavioral and Brain Sciences*, vol. 7, no. 4, 1984.) What we are most interested in here is the expression of associationism in Skinner's theory of behaviour.

Probably Skinner's most important contribution in this respect is his recognition of two distinct forms of behaviour. A *respondent* is behaviour elicited by stimuli, as in classical conditioning, i.e. a reflex. But there is also another class of behaviours called *operants*, which are not elicited by stimuli, but are emitted by a variety of other causes. The organism orginally has a large pool of these uncommitted operants. Their expression has consequences, however, and these consequences may raise or lower the probability of subsequent responding. Such consequences are thus called either reinforcers or punishers, and the various patterns of responses related to them are known as the *contingencies* of reinforcement or punishment. Finally, the consequences of responding are typically associated with particular stimuli. An oft-used example is that of our behaviour at traffic lights: the consequences of depressing the accelerator when they are green are different from those which follow when they are red (cf. Catania 1984). Thus, stimuli come to define the consequences, and thereby to control the operant. Instead of the simple dual association between stimulus and response, then, we have a three-way association between *stimulus, response* and *consequence*. This reflects, but extends, Thorndike's Law of Effect, but contrasts with the simple Law of Exercise favoured by Pavlov, Watson and many others.

Understandably, in the light of his scientific strategy, Skinner was loath to express these associations in any more expansive form. Indeed, he occasionally ridiculed notions like 'the strength of a bond, or the conductivity of a neural pathway, or the excitatory potential of a habit' as 'the use of theory as a refuge from the data' (Skinner 1984, p. 517). The proper business of a science of behaviour is to evaluate the *probability of response* and the observable conditions which determine it. Since we can dispense with theory, we don't need a hypothetico-deductive methodology (see Chapter 1). All we need is an empirical (inductive) description of the conditions determining the probability of a response. All mental events – thoughts, beliefs, perceptions, etc. – can be contained by descriptions of controlling stimuli and the histories of contingencies of reinforcement responsible for that control. There is little need for concepts of entities or processes underlying observable behaviour and hypothesised to give rise to it.

More recent behaviourism

The above are illustrations of theories based on associationism, within a behaviourist perspective, prominent throughout the first half of this century. There were many more in the same period, and there have been others in the period since. These do not seem to have involved any *different* or more elaborate expressions of associationism, however. Rather, they have been chiefly concerned with the discovery of further principles or 'laws' governing conditioning (whether of the respondent or operant type) and with the extension of these into new areas. For instance, Hull (1943) introduced a number of postulates concerning the role of motivation, particularly drive or drive reduction, in the strength of the S-R connection, (or 'habit' as he preferred to call it). He also introduced the idea of secondary reinforcers – a class of reinforcers such as social approval or money whose effectiveness arises out of prior association (i.e. as conditioned reinforcers) with the primary reinforcers (e.g. food, warmth) they are useful in procuring. This was an idea taken up by Spence (1956), and was used by others in the explanation of 'higher-order' social behaviour in humans. An up-to-date account of research on laws of association, from within the framework of conditioning, is provided by Mackintosh (1983), who also explains how recent criticisms have led to better approaches to conditioning and learning than the theories of Watson, Pavlov and others would have suggested possible. But since these – as already suggested – have not elaborated on the nature of associations *per se* (so much as what is associated with what in, e.g., CS-UCS, UR-UCR connections) we now leave this discussion. Instead, we turn to movements over the last twenty years that have attempted to restore some of the 'mind' to psychology, via some of the pre-behaviourist notions of association.

Neo-associationism

Of course, movements had already been developing within behaviourism itself in reaction to the simple associationism of S-R psychology. For instance, Tolman cited experiments in which rats were allowed to explore a maze for several trials, but without any reward in the food-box; if food was then introduced, the rats' subsequent running from the start to the food-box was as error-free as that of rats that had been trained with food reward from trial 1. In other experiments, rats that had been trained to swim a maze for food were then found to be able to run just as quickly, even though this entailed the use of different movements (responses) (Tolman 1948). This seemed to suggest that the behaving animal acquires not simply new responses or reflexes, but rather new 'knowledge' about the environment (Tolman spoke of cognitive 'maps'). A little later, the new postulates of secondary reinforcement 'sounded the death knell of primitive behaviourism', as Mowrer (1960, p. 78) put it. Tolman had emphasised that human movements are 'molar' responses, in the sense of involving numerous muscles, in flexible combination and complex sequences, rather than discrete muscle contractions.

Karl Lashley, meanwhile, was doing ablation studies in which parts of the brains of conditioned rats were excised to assess which parts, or how much, of the brain was critically involved in the S-R association. These experiments suggested retention of the conditioned response even after complete removal of the motor cortex or of large areas of the visual cortex. Lashley's conclusion is now a classic:

> It is difficult to interpret such conclusions but I think they point to the conclusion that the associative connections or memory traces of the conditioned reflex do not extend across the cortex as well-defined arcs or pathways. Such arcs are either diffused through all parts of the cortex, pass by relay through lower centres, or do not exist.
>
> (Lashley 1951, p. 500)

A growing body of opinion was thus already pointing to the deficiencies of behaviourism, and turning 'inward' again to central processes and mental states.

In the last two decades, many new associationistic ideas have been introduced. Most are unashamedly mentalistic, some concerned chiefly with memory, but more general concerns are to be found as well; most, but not all, being expressed in terms of, or having, close affiliations with, the language of computers (or information processing). None of these has become sufficiently established to have become a 'main line', like the work of Thorndike or Pavlov, and new ideas are emerging all the time. Many of these have actually become 'constructivist' expressions (see next chapter). This makes an exhaustive review even less appropriate. We shall have to be content therefore with a few glimpses at these new associationistic expressions.

The 'neo-associationists' as they have been called (Anderson and Bower 1973) have been much more liberal with their 'connections', and about *what* becomes connected, than their predecessors. Part of this is due in no small part to the arrival of the computer as a way of modelling the human mind. As Anderson and Bower (1973, p. 38) explained:

> For these tasks, for theories about the structure of memory and the nature of language comprehension, the clear theoretical leaders in the past decade have been the small number of computer scientists who work on models of mental organisation. In our opinion, it is these computer simulation models of mental memory that begin to actualise the full potential of associationism as a theory of mental organisation.

But it is an actualisation in no small way determined by the nature of the medium – i.e. the computer – itself. Wilson (1980) identifies several ways in which neo-associationists differ from the behaviourists. Perhaps the most critical assumption is that, like the earlier associationists, they are prepared to hypothesise associations between 'mental events' – e.g. representations, symbols, concepts or propositions – which are not primitive stimuli or responses, and which do not correspond directly with objects and events in the outside world. And neo-associationists have not been afraid to posit innate structures when these seemed appropriate. This freedom has corresponded with the language and mechanistic quality of computers, and also the rich interconnectedness of brain structures, to permit the development of many so-called 'network' or 'connectionist' models of memory. These are the high water-mark of contemporary associationism.

Among the earliest such models were those of Fiegenbaum (1963) and Hintzman (1968). These models involved the learning of nonsense syllables as paired associates, or in serial learning, *using a discrimination net*. This sorts each complex stimulus according to its attribute values (e.g. for a nonsense syllable, each letter in each position), until the stimulus is passed to a node (storage location in memory). This node then generates a response cue which forms the association to the 'correct' response.

These early associative models were very simple, and mimicked several aspects of learning and memory, but there were obvious differences. For example, a stimulus remained associated with one, and only one, response, which is not like human memory. Nor does it allow for the many different kinds of 'semantic' knowledge in memory, entailing many different kinds of relations (cf. Anderson and Bower 1973).

Quillian (1969) devised a network model of linguistic processing in memory (called Teachable Language Comprehender – or TLC) which overcame some of these problems by employing 'labelled associations' to represent the qualities of these relations. In this model all information is encoded in memory either as a 'unit' or as a 'property'. A unit is a concept of an object or event (i.e. a representation of a whole category of things such as 'cup', 'shoes', etc.). A property is anything that might be said about a unit (e.g. red, shaggy, fast, furious (dog) that belongs to (John)). In this case there are not only associations or 'pointers' between unit dog and each of these – and presumably many other – properties, but also between unit dog and John. So there is another association here, too. Moreover, new concepts can be formed in memory by associations, in experience, between old concepts (for example, John's dog's veterinary surgeon), each of which will have pointers to properties that thus become nested in each other. As Anderson and Bower (1973, p. 81) explain: 'Since there is no limit to the number and nesting of properties that can be associated to a given unit, it is clear that concepts and predicates of practically unbounded complexity could be built up and represented in the memory format.'

We will not discuss here the processes suggested by Quillian by which these associations emerge, but it is important to mention the nesting of properties in what are called super-set relations, which were conceived in order to simplify the structuring of information. An example would be that shown in Figure 3.1, in which general properties (e.g. has four legs, tail, etc.) of the subordinate concepts of dog, are stored only once with the superordinate, rather than with each and every subordinate. In this way a property

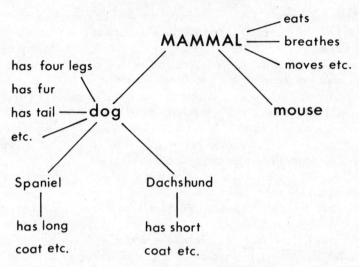

Figure 3.1   A nested network such as that of Collins and Quillian (Quillian, 1969)

applicable to a concept need not be associated with every instance, but can none the less be 'found' through association with the superordinate.

Thus the associations in Quillian's model are 'labelled' relations like 'is a' (as in 'a dog *is a* mammal'), 'has a', 'can', and so on, as well as conjunctives (like 'John's dog') and some others. These display relational qualities which are quite different from the associations of the behaviourists and of the philosophical associationists. It is important to note that it is a model of what a computer does in processing a sentence; it is thus a possible model of *what* the human mind has to do in processing and responding to similar stimuli. But the use of *de facto* labels glosses over the question of how these relations are established in the first place.

Quillian's model had the virtue of generating hypotheses which could be experimentally tested. Refinements by his colleagues Collins and Loftus (1975) which proposed (through a 'spreading activation' model) that some links or associations have different strengths, and operate faster, according to frequency of use have also been tested. But the empirical evidence, in support of either model, has not so far been substantial.

Another example of network modelling is Anderson and Bower's (1973) Human Associative Memory (HAM). Like earlier associationists these authors envisage associations forming between 'semantic primitives' (i.e. simple 'ideas') to form complex ideas, which in turn can be associated. From these, however, propositional structures (e.g. statements, assertions) can be stored to form a higher order of analysis. These are the basic units of knowledge in HAM. They take the form of 'propositional trees' in which the nodes are the ideas (e.g. dog, person) and the links are the associations.

These trees are what are input to memory. 'HAM will attempt to store these trees in long-term memory by forming associations corresponding to each of the links in the tree' (p. 169). And since nodes can belong to more than one proposition, the trees intersect. Thus, knowledge in HAM consists of a vast network of such intersecting trees. But, as with the Quillian model, the associations are not *just* associations in the traditional sense, but also cues which capture the *quality* of the relation. 'The ordered association corresponds to the traditional association in that it expresses a functional connection between the ideas, a and b (i.e. that a can lead to b), but with the added specification that a will lead to b only if the relation X is evoked' (p. 181). These relations are essentially qualifiers like fact, context, predicate, location, time, object, and so on. Given a verbal, visual or other input, the mind identifies the idea *a*, say, and the relation X (e.g. one of those above), and returns an ordered list of all nodes (concepts) *b* that correspond.

Again, it has to be stressed that this is a model conceived for computer simulation, and whether or how the mind stores associations like this is a different question. In particular, while it is relatively easy to envisage the abstraction and storage of associations based on contiguity or succession, say (such that the experience of one item automatically evokes or is followed by another), it is much more difficult to envisage how this actually happens in the case of associations of the form 'is a', 'has a', 'can', and so on. The use of labelled associations side-steps what seems to be the crucial problem in how knowledge is formed and used. None the less, network models of this kind have been extremely heuristic in the sense of helping psychologists envisage new possibilities. For instance, Anderson and Bower (1973) suggest that although there is no innate knowledge in their model, in the sense of prior associations among memory nodes, a system of this type definitely requires some 'innate primitives' as a starting point. This fertility of neo-associationism has led to further theories in recent years which have attempted to get us much nearer to what actually goes on in the brain mind. We will now attempt to illustrate these briefly.

Parallel distributed processing (PDP)

It is now clear that information processing in the computer is different from that in the human brain in several ways. For instance, the computer is very good at doing things like arithmetic, or handling large numbers or specific items, or specified associations, with extreme reliability; but it is very poor at reaching conclusions from partial or 'noisy' information, such as human brains do all the time in perceiving the three-dimensional world around us, or predicting the total structure of partially occluded objects (Hinton and Anderson 1981). On the other hand, the computer carries out its information processing extremely quickly even though it does so in more or less fixed sequential steps. The passage of information along nerve fibres is around a thousand times slower than in the 'wires' of a computer, even though the brain can do many things, like interpreting sentences of speech, a great deal more quickly than the computer. This has led to the conclusion that the computational processes in the brain are different in kind from those in the computer, and to the suggestion that the separate steps in information processing in the brain must be to a large extent carried out in *parallel* in the brain, and that the knowledge on which it operates must be, to a correspond-ing extent, multiply represented, or *distributed*. Many recent theories of higher mental processes and knowledge representation have been based on this idea of parallel distributed processing. Only the barest features of these theories will be presented here; for overall reviews see Hinton and Anderson (1981); Rumelhart, McClelland and the PDP Research Group (1986); and McClelland, Rumelhart and the PDP Research Group (1986).

The basic structure of models of this type, then, usually consists of a large set of interconnected 'processors' (analogues of neurons or sets of neurons in the brain) which are highly interconnected and interact with each other through excitatory or inhibitory discharges along their connections. The processors are 'simple' in the sense of responding to quite simple features or attributes of stimuli. Instead of simple and complex 'ideas' forming by *specific* associations between *specific* units, these correspond with *patterns* of activity distributed over many processor units. Instead of an individual signal passing between individual units – e.g. between the vision and olfaction of a rose, or between parts of a sequence of movements – there is association between activity patterns, 'bringing together and interconnecting the various parts of the pattern' (Kohonen Lehtio and Oja 1981, p. 108).

Although this associationism is still based on changing connections be-tween units, instead of S-S or S-R associations, we have Sp-Sp or Sp-Rp associations, where the 'p' subscript stands for 'patterns of activity'. This simple fact of distribution of activity in patterns across units engenders some surprising properties, when compared with traditional associationist models. First it means that damage to isolated parts of the system will not necessarily damage or destroy the knowledge base (recall the observations of Lashley mentioned earlier in this chapter). It also means that the system is better equipped to deal with noisy or incomplete information, in the sense that it can 'make more of' such information. Parallel distributed processing can also, potentially, account for certain puzzles about concept formation. You may recall how, since Aristotle, it had been more or less accepted that concepts like 'flower', 'house', etc. were formed by abstraction of common features (petals, sepals, stalk, etc.). Over the last twenty years it has become clear that the mental representations of concepts are not as simple as this. In particular, some members of concepts seem to be better, or more typical, members than

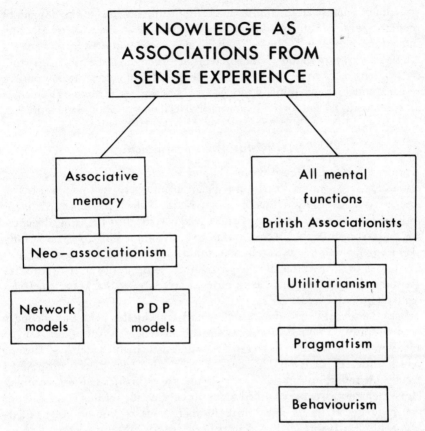

Figure 3.2   Some expressions of associationism in contemporary theory

others, with one particular member – the 'prototype' – being the best of all (see Neisser 1987 for reviews). Parallel distributed processing (PDP) can help explain this 'graded structure' of concepts. And it can also help explain the formation of abstract rules, because recurring regularities between patterns of activities can themselves be registered in the form of emergent patterns of activity. Not surprisingly, therefore, PDP has been seen to be applicable to areas more general than passive memory storage, to include perception, conception, motor production and other 'emergent properties' of the mind. Interested readers are thus urged to go to the original literature for details of the ingredients and scope of PDP models.

In sum, a major branch of associationism (neo-associationism) has emerged in the last twenty years or so, in reaction to behaviourism. This new branch has become more 'mental' by specifically modelling internal proces-ses, usually in the form of a computer program. Theoretically, the first main consequence has been to confine associations, once again, to the domain of memory, whilst allowing rationalist principles and processes to govern other operations of the mind. The second has been the development from these of a whole new class of models which may have turned out to be more constructivist in character than associationist. Meanwhile, of course, behaviourism remains a prominent strand in modern psychology, so that associationism is far from being a spent force. A summary of its history is shown in Figure 3.2.

Criticisms of associationism

As mentioned at the outset of this chapter, the other 'pillar' of psychology, classical rationalism, has also been associationism's perpetual antagonist. The basic argument of rationalists, you may recall, is that human knowledge is too rich to be derived from experience, which is 'fuzzy', unreliable, degenerate, and so on. In reply, associationists ask: how, then, did such wonderfully rich knowledge *arrive* in the human mind? (As pointed out at the end of Chapter 2, to say that the knowledge is 'innate' is not really an answer to this question.) So associationists, as empiricists, have argued that knowledge *must* come from experience.

Rationalists have replied to this in turn by arguing that prior knowledge is needed simply to make *sense* of sense experience. Associationists have accepted this in various degrees. Aristotle postulated a faculty of reason, which imposed 'form' on sense data. The British associationists proposed a faculty of 'reflection' by which simple ideas were associated into complex ideas. Behaviourists have tended to vary considerably on this issue, though generally declaring its irrelevance to their laws of conditioning. Neo-associationists have tended to be more like Aristotle in confining the sphere of associations to knowledge storage in memory, whilst admitting the presence of some innate 'primitives' and processes operating on sense data. Finally, theorists of parallel distributed processing have confessed to being quite agnostic on this nature–nurture issue, because structure readily emerges out of the pattern of inputs to highly interconnected units, out of the pattern of interconnections among these units and between these and effectors (see Rumelhart, McClelland and the PDP Research Group 1986).

That associationism is incapable of explaining the richness and versatility of our knowledge is easily the most general criticism, but it is not one that you can accept or reject very easily. As with all scientific theory, acceptance and rejection depend on a wide range of determinants, some scientific, some not. There is no 'critical experiment'; but there are further criticisms, and we must look at these further before we decide which, if any, version of associationism we find acceptable.

As we have seen, associationism consists of a diversity of formulations of a very simple idea – that associations in nature are 'mirrored' by associations in the mind. 'An *association* is simply two or more entities which are linked so that elicitation of one can lead to elicitation of the other' (Wilson 1980, p. 105). Thus, associationism is 'mechanistic', in the sense that knowledge and thought are governed by simple 'push–pull' processes: if *a* occurs frequently with *b* in nature, presentation of *a* will evoke *b* in the mind; if *a* is succeeded by *b* and then by *c*, then presentation of *a* will evoke this train. Successful adaptation to the environment (this seen as a relatively constant set of conditions) consists of the formation of a corresponding set of 'habits'. We can see attractions of this mechanistic view where the desire to 'predict and control' people, as in behaviourism, is our goal; but how realistic and useful is it as a model of the human mind?

The most fundamental criticism here is that it entails a misleading model of nature. Nature is more complex than regularly associated features, objects and events; and so, therefore, is our sense experience. The world we experience with our senses is constantly changing in space and time, and almost always novel, and only rarely are juxtapositions or successions of sense data the same on different occasions. This is essentially the argument put at the beginning of Chapter 2, which seemed to make classical rationalism a necessity. Not surprisingly, therefore, the best illustration of 'real' experience, and its mismatch with associationist models, is that of human language, as put by the staunchest of modern rationalists, Noam Chomsky (see Chapter 2). But much the same can be said of our moment-to-moment perceptions of the world, our motor behaviour on it, and so on, all of which appear to be constantly variable, and multiply determined, rather than consisting of repetitive associations. In other words, associationism appears to be based on a misleadingly simple view of the world.

Many other criticisms of associationism flow from this point. For instance, *when* stimuli, features, objects, etc. occur together or in succession, they can do so in one of a whole range of sensible relationships – by location, by membership of the same class, by action of one upon the other, and so on. But *all* are presumed to be represented by one and the same kind of association. Thus, there is little structure in the associations of traditional associationism. The more recent neo-associationists have been conscious of this problem, but have 'solved' it only by labelling, in their models, the *de facto* relations identified in nature. As Anderson and Bower (1973, p. 25) explained: 'All recent attempts to simulate human memory with an associative model have had to resort to labelling the associative links with the various relations they express.' As mentioned earlier, this is identifying part of what the mind must do in forming knowledge, without indicating how it is done.

A further problem arising from a simplified model of nature is that, when mirrored in the human, the model becomes utterly stultifying. There are few indications in associative models of the mind of how new knowledge can be generated from existing knowledge in a way that is so characteristic of human creativity and flexibility. As Anderson and Bower (1973, p. 25) also explain: 'To this day there is no well worked out theory of how the mind spontaneously interrogates its own knowedge to construct new knowledge.'

It is possible that the more recent PDP models will overcome some of these problems. But these are such a radical departure from all previous associationism that they might be better described as 'contructivist' theories, which are the subject of the next chapter. In line with this, Hinton, McClelland and Rumelhart (1986) have put the three important features of distributed representations as: '(a) their essentially constructive character; (b) their ability to generalise automatically to novel situations; and (c) their tunability to changing environments' (p. 79). But this is a highly controversial issue. A number of authors have argued recently that 'connectionism' amounts largely to an attempt to pursue the traditional goals of behaviourism under another guise. See, for example, contributions in Costall and Still (1987), and the special issue of the journal *Cognition* (vol. 28, Nos. 1–2, 1988), devoted to critiques of PDP theories. 'Perhaps the most salient common theme in these papers is that many connectionist proposals . . . seem to be tied more closely to an agenda of reviving associationism as a central doctrine of learning and mental functions' (Pinker and Mehler 1988, pp. 1–2). You might be in a better position to decide on this matter after you have read the next chapter.

One of the problems we criticised rationalist theories about, in Chapter 2, was the weakness of the empirical evidence in support of them. This is not a problem with associationist theories; there is abundant empirical evidence that humans, as well as other animals, *can* form associations in the way that theories predict. This evidence is strongest in behaviourist experiments. The question is: what is it all evidence *of*? The fact that people appear to be sensitive to correlations in experience does not necessarily mean that these are of the simple S-S or S-R type; nor that this is *all* that the human mind is capable of. It is one thing to argue that a simple model is predictive of behaviour in certain (predictable) situations, but quite another to infer that this is how the mind or brain works in governing *all* behaviour in *all* situations. There are suggestions in comparative studies of associationistic learning across species that the 'extra' brain volume that humans and primates have relative to, say, reptiles and fishes is of little import, because the latter appear to 'learn' almost as effectively as the former. As Oakley (1985) put it: 'Though the idea that learning depends on neocortex has a long history, there is one serious objection to it, namely, that comparative learning studies show that neocortex is manifestly *not* a prerequisite for learning' (p. 155); and 'Conventional learning designs of the sort employed in psychology laboratories then give rather few clues as to the unique selective advantages conferred by neocortex which might account for its emergence in the course of vertebrate evolution' (p. 167). This of course suggests that there is something radically wrong with our (associationist) conception of learning.

Whereas rationalism has 'rich' theories which are difficult to prove (or disprove), then, the problem with associationism is that its theories tend to be so thin as to be trivially supported, empirically. It can probably be said, in fact, that where richer associationist theories have emerged (as in neo-associationist memory theories), empirical support has been more equivocal, or (as with PDP theories) they may have begun to depart from associationism altogether.

Of course, refutations of simple (particularly behaviouristic) associationism, to the effect that there are other (central) processes operating also, is manifest in a range of experiments, at least since the time of Tolman. Some of these were mentioned above. Such counter-evidence against the 'evidence' of behaviourist experiments was a major impetus to the revival of 'cognitive' theories, whether these be based on rationalism (with or without admixtures of associationism), or constructivism, which we will turn to in the next chapter.

Finally, it has to be remembered that behaviourism, as a special branch of associationism, reflects a peculiar philosophy of science which has always been controversial, and has been frequently criticised for its dehumanising and manipulative undertones. Since these do not bear directly on associationism *per se*, we will not deal with these here, but discuss them briefly in Chapter 6.

References

Anderson, J.R. and Bower, G.H. (1973) *Human Associative Memory*. Washington, Hemisphere Publishing.

Bolles, R.C. (1975) *Learning Theory*. New York, Holt, Rinehart & Winston.

Catania, A.C. (1984) Introduction. *The Behavioural and Brain Sciences*, 7, 473.

Collins, A.M. and Loftus, E.F. (1975) A spreading activation model of semantic processing. *Psychological Review*, 82, 407–28.

Costall, A. and Still, A. (eds.) (1987) *Cognitive Psychology in Question*. New York, St. Martin's Press.

Fiegenbaum, E.A. (1963) Simulation of verbal learning behaviour. In E.A. Fiegenbaum and J. Feldman (eds.), *Computers and Thought*. New York, McGraw-Hill.

Hinton, G.E. and Anderson, J.A. (eds.) (1981) *Parallel Models of Associative Memory*. Hillsdale, Lawrence Erlbaum.

Hinton, G.E., McClelland, J.L. and Rumelhart, D.E. (1986) Distributed representations. In D.E. Rumelhart, J.L. McClelland and the PDP Research Group, *Parallel Distributed Processing Vol. 1. Foundations*. Cambridge, Massachusetts, MIT Press.

Hintzman, D.L. (1968) Explorations with a discrimination net model for paired-associate learning. *Journal of Mathematical Psychology*, 5, 123–62.

Hull, C.L. (1943) *Principles of Behavior*. New York, Appleton.

Hyman, A. and Walsh, J. (eds.) (1973) *Philosophy in the Middle Ages*. Indianapolis, Hackett.

James, W. (1890/1950) *Principles of Psychology*. New York, Dover Publications.

Johnston, A. (1965) *Francis Bacon*. London, Batsford.

Kohonen, J., Lehtio, P. and Oja, E. (1981) Storage and processing of information in distributed associative memory systems. In G.E. Hinton and J.A. Anderson (eds.), *Parallel Models of Associative Memory*. Hillsdale, Lawrence Erlbaum.

Laird, J. (1932/1967) *Hume's Philosophy of Human Nature*. London, Archon Books.

Lashley, K. (1951) In search of the engram. *Symposia of the Society of Experimental Biology*, 4, 454–582.

Leahey, T.H. (1987) *A History of Psychology*. Englewood Cliffs, Prentice-Hall.

McClelland, J.L., Rumelhart, D.E. and the PDP Research Group (1986) *Parallel Distributed Processing: Explorations in the Microstructure of Cognition*, Vol. 2, Psychological and Biological Models. Cambridge, Mass., MIT Press.

Mackintosh, N.J. (1983) *Conditioning and Associative Learning*. Oxford, Clarendon Press.

Morgan, C.L. (1984) *An Introduction to Comparative Psychology*. London, Scott.

Mowrer, O.H. (1960) *Learning Theory and Behaviour*. New York, Wiley.

Neisser, U. (ed.) (1987) *Concepts and Conceptual Development*. Cambridge, Cambridge University Press.

Oakley, D.A. (1985) Cerebral cortex and adaptive behaviour. In D.A. Oakley and H.C. Plotkin (eds.), *Brain, Behaviour and Evolution*. London, Methuen.

Peters, R.S. (1956) *Hobbes*. Harmondsworth, Penguin.

Pinker, S. and Mehler, J. (1988) Introduction. *Cognition*, 28, 1–2.

Popkin, R.H. (1966) *The Philosophy of the Sixteenth and Seventeenth Centuries*. New York, Free Press.

Quillian, M.R. (1969) The teachable language comprehender. *Communications of the Association for Computing Machinery*, 12, 459–76.

Robinson, D.N. (1981) *An Intellectual History of Psychology*. New York, Macmillan.

Rumelhart, D.E., McClelland, J.L. and the PDP Research Group (1986) *Parallel Distributed Processing: Explorations in the Microstructure of Cognition*, Vol. 1, Foundations. Cambridge, Mass., MIT Press.

Skinner, B.F. (1984) Responses. *The Behavioral and Brain Sciences*, 7, 517.

Smith, E.E. and Medin, D.L. (1981) *Categories and Concepts*. Cambridge, Mass., Harvard University Press.

Spence, K.W. (1956) *Behaviour Theory and Conditioning*. New Haven, Yale University Press.

Thorndike, E.L. (1898/1911) *Animal Intelligence*. New York, Macmillan.

Tolman, E.C. (1938) The determiners of behavior at a choice point. *Psychological Review*, 5, 1–41.

Tolman, E.C. (1948) Cognitive maps in rats and men. *Psychological Review*, 55, 189–208.

Watson, J.B. (1913) Psychology as the behaviourist views it. *Psychological Review*, 20, 158–77.

Wilson, K.V. (1980) *From Associations to Structure*. Amsterdam, North Holland.

Yolton, J.W. (1977) *The Locke Reader: Selections from the Works of John Locke*. Cambridge, Cambridge University Press.

4

Constructivism

Most people would acknowledge that a wholly new, alternative view of the working of the human mind was conceived by Immanuel Kant (*Critique of Pure Reason*, 1781, and other works). In philosophy, the effect of his work was astounding: 'All philosophy before 1781 seems to flow into Kant's great system and little that has appeared since cannot be traced back to his influence' (Wolf 1968, p. xi); but its effect on psychology has been very great, too, if rather more indirectly than the effects of our previous two schools. As with these other two schools, though, and as with all great issues and ideas in psychology, Kant's contribution hinged on the nature of knowledge.

Kant had found himself in a state of despair after reading Hume's claims that certain knowledge (based, as Hume believed, purely on associations of synchrony or succession) is impossible. Thus, he turned against raw associationism. But he also turned against rationalist explanations of knowledge.

> The 'Critique of Pure Reason' consists in showing how reason comes to grief when it tries to give us knowledge that transcends the phenomenal world. In particular, Kant seeks to demolish what he calls rational psychology . . . No claims to offer us rational knowledge of the soul, the world as a whole, or God are tenable.
>
> (Kaufmann 1980, p. 101)

But Kant did not 'do away' with experience as the source of knowledge; nor did he do away with innate sources of knowledge. Instead, he brought the two together in a new synthesis that was aimed to solve the problems they created, and so to reconcile the antagonism between them. Put simply, Kant argued that the world we know is *constructed* by the human mind.

It is important to point out the difficulties, self-contradictions and sheer obscurantism of much of Kant's writings on this subject. All we can do here is sketch an outline that seems most important to us as psychologists. First of all, Kant asserted and argued that we could not have coherent experience without innate (a priori) concepts. 'Otherwise it would be possible for appearances to crowd in upon the soul, and be such as would never allow of experience . . . and consequently would be for us as good as nothing' (quoted by Walsh 1968, p. 62). So experiences need to be 'tied together' in some lawful, universally applicable ways, otherwise objective knowledge could not be possible. Thus, Kant proposed that knowledge has two distinct components. The first is a set of a priori concepts, or categories: these are logically different kinds of quantity, of quality, of relation and of modality. It is important to stress the purely *logical* content of these concepts – in the sense that they each contain functions that are logically necessary; to deny what they define leads directly to nonsense. For instance, nothing can happen without a reason of some sort; and nothing can vanish 'clean out of existence'. The pure categories of the mind merely assert logically necessary truths; but they are not knowledge of the world in their own right. This is what distinguishes them from the a priori knowledge of the rationalist.

What the categories do, according to Kant, is to make coherent knowledge from experience *possible*. Thus, he introduced the notion of the schema – a mental construction of experience which reflects both the real world of ever-variable objects and events *and* the underlying logic of the categories as imposed on that experience. As Walsh (1968, p. 82) puts it: 'the schema of a category is, in effect, a second concept which has the advantage over the category in its abstract form of being directly cashable in terms of sense experience, and can yet be plausibly thought to provide an interpretation of it.'

Thus, there are two kinds of concepts: a priori concepts, and empirical concepts. What is a concept? A concept is a rule of combination or synthesis which brings various representations together under one representation. An empirical concept arises from the senses through organised comparison with previous sense experience, but by more than a process of abstraction in the associationistic sense: 'The form of a concept, as a discursive representation, is always constructed' (cf. Schroder 1968, p. 137).

In this way – by tying in sense experience with universal, intersubjective and necessary laws of thought – Kant thought that he had solved the problem of objective knowledge. Not all philosophers since have agreed, but we will not go into that. What we have to recognise is the role that Kant played in bringing the idea of the schema, the importance of concepts and the general principle of constructivism into psychology. As before, the purpose of this chapter is to illustrate expressions of this idea in the twentieth century, and then to subject them to some criticism.

Gestalt psychology

The transcendentalism and idealism that followed Kant, most notably in the writings of Hegel and Goethe, pervaded German philosophy and psychology in the nineteenth and early twentieth centuries, and spread to more distant parts in Europe and North América. A psychological influence arising at the turn of this century, and one still felt today, is that expressed by the so-called 'Gestaltists'. These were a group of psychologists, originating in Germany, but later moving to North America, who with their followers constituted a major 'school' or movement of psychology, right up to the 1940s and 1950s.

The movement started with the interpretation of some dramatic perceptual phenomena, rather than as a distinct, coherent theory. For instance, Ehrenfels had argued in 1890 that the perception of melody involved a 'form quality' that transcends the sum of its particular elements. But the real founder of the Gestalt movement is Max Wertheimer, whose studies of the perception of movement were first published in 1912. The subject of these studies was the 'Phi' phenomenon.

We have all experienced the 'Phi' phenomenon whenever we perceive apparent motion when two or more lights close together are illuminated in rapid succession. Wertheimer worked with two stripes placed on a wall in a darkened room a few inches apart, which could be rapidly illuminated, one after the other. When this happens the experimental subject in the room reports, not two stripes apart, but a single stripe that moves in the direction of the order of illumination. As Robinson (1981, p. 414) describes it:

> The important point is this: nothing in the experimental arrangement, except the phenomenon itself, would lead to the prediction of apparent motion. That is, there is no physical feature of the environment that permits the prediction of the effect. A purely stimulus-bound description of the laboratory setting will be devoid of any allusion to movement. The motion is created by the observer.

There was obviously something other than raw sense experience involved here; there were obviously built-in, lawful, mental processes that imposed organisation on sense data to produce orderly percepts (gestalts). So reasoned the Gestalt psychologists. Wertheimer's students, such as Koffka and Kohler, went on to reveal and demonstrate these mental 'laws' in a number of famous perceptual phenomena. These include the law of closure, as in the perception of a complete triangle in Figure 4.1, and the law of proximity, as in the perception of columns, rather than separate lines, in Figure 4.2.

Kohler was interned on the island of Tenerife during the First World War, and turned his attentions to problem-solving among the island's apes. Chimps were presented with food which was too high for them to reach, but boxes had also been placed in the cage. By stacking these, one upon the other, the chimps managed to reach the food. In another study, food was placed outside the cage, and the chimps were provided with two sticks, neither of which alone was long enough to reach the food. But the sticks could slot together, and, after a period of examination, a chimp would suddenly do just that, and thus reach the food.

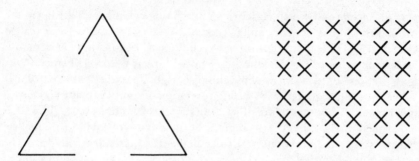

Figure 4.1   The law of closure   Figure 4.2   The law of proximity

Such 'insight', according to Kohler, was due to the same processes in apes as it is in humans: an active reconstruction of sense data. Later Gestaltists, in the 1940s and 1950s turned their attention to human problem-solving as a constructive reorganisation of problem situations. In all of these and many other endeavours, the Kantian undercurrent was there, in the sense of logical relations imposed upon sense data to construct a 'world' in representation. A brief recent review of the far-reaching goals of Gestalt psychology can be found in Arnheim (1986).

Bartlett and remembering

In his well-known book *Remembering* (1932), Bartlett described studies in which subjects were asked to reproduce textual and pictorial materials which they had earlier experienced (describing or depicting a sequence of events as in a story or narrative). He found that his subjects typically elaborated or distorted the original facts, and they seemed to do this in a way which imposed their personal and social conventions over the story. Thus, he concluded that remembering is a *reconstructive* as well as a *reproductive* process – an interaction between the facts of experience and some abstract cognitive representation of the world. Bartlett used the word 'schema' to describe the latter, and is thus frequently described as 'the acknowledged originator of the use of schemata to describe story recall' (Thorndyke 1984, p. 144). As such he is the forerunner of modern laboratory studies of schemata which we will describe below.

It should be obvious that, although the title of Bartlett's book suggests that it is about memory, it is, in fact, about much more than that. Through the study of the process of remembering he hoped to reveal not simply retrieval from a long-term store, but also the united functions of mentality in general, including personal (affective) and social factors.

Thus, Bartlett's use of the term 'schema' was a very broad one indeed, and was meant to include socially derived attitudes and feelings as well as cognitions; he was concerned about the possible narrowness implicit in the term, in fact (see Edwards and Middleton 1987). But it was clear that he saw the *function* of an abstract schema as a way of liberating us from the strictures of immediate experience. As he later put it in his book on *Thinking* (1958, p. 200):

> It is with thinking as it is with recall: Memory and all the life of images and words which goes with it are one with . . . the development of constructive imagination and constructive thought wherein at length we find the most complete release from the narrowness of present time and space.

Child development theories

Constructivism has been particularly prominent in child development theory, and it is here that we find some of the most famous names in psychology. Their theories tend to have been so rich and elaborate that it is impossible to provide a satisfactory brief summary. All we shall do, then, is provide brief outlines of the theories of Piaget, Bruner and Vygotsky to indicate their constructivist qualities.

Jean Piaget

For Piaget, human mentality is part of a continuum of adaptation of organic life to its environments which, for each individual, starts in biology and ends in knowledge. This process is one which, according to Piaget, is replete with constructivism. Even the developmental adaption of the physical structures of organisms is *epigenetic*, in the sense of involving interactions between genes and environment so that the most adaptive structures result. Likewise with mental structures: these cannot be traced to innate instructions, nor to associationistic 'copies' of the environment.

The child appears to be born with a few simple reflexes, like the sucking reflex and the palmar reflex; but these are not fixed mechanical 'automations', or structures there for all time. They are already complex developmental schemas. Thus, an infant may suck a thumb as well as the mother's breast. The thumb-sucking is thereby assimilated into this sucking schema, which itself changes, or accommodates, to the new sensations produced by the infant's actions. This equilibrium between assimilation and accommodation thus results in a more generalised structure, or schema. The palmar reflex also becomes integrated into a 'grasping' schema.

By similar processes, always stemming from the child's actions, such structural adaptations themselves become co-ordinated, and new structures are constructed, of progressively more general scope. The 'looking' schema and the 'grasping' schema become co-ordinated into one of many sensory-motor schemas (hand-eye co-ordination). The construction of the 'structures' known as object permanence provides a further illustration. At first there is no differentiation between the sense data and the looking schema. The existence of the object is undifferentiated from the action of looking at it – the two are fused; this is the young infant's *knowledge* of the object. When an object disappears behind a chair, say, it ceases to exist. But further action (bodily movements co-ordinated with looking elsewhere) reveals translations or displacements (rather than disappearances) of the object. And these can be represented as the schema known as 'the group of translations' (sometimes called 'the group of displacements').

It is important to recognise how this 'structure' involves the co-ordination of actions. Now, if the object is a ball which rolls from point A, and disappears at point B, the child 'knows' to look for it at point C $(A - B - C)$, whereas previously he or she would have looked at A. Or if it rolls from point A, bounces off point B and ends up at point C, the child 'knows' that he or she need not follow the precise trajectory to retrieve it; he or she can go directly to C (i.e. ABC, or $AC = AB + BC$). Now the knowledge is quite different, and imparts new powers to the child. As well as *combinativity* $(AB + BC = AC)$ there is also *reversibility* $(AB + BA = 0)$. In particular, the object and the subject's body become independent entities, and there is a whole transformation of attitude to the world (Piaget 1970).

Between 2 years and almost 6–7 years, children go through a similar sequence with these structures as they have just gone through with their sensory-motor structures. There is a parallel, in that co-ordination of structures leads to the representation of invariants: but now these invariants are at a higher, or more abstract, level. In the sensory-motor stage the child's representations are still tied to particular actions with particular objects. In the next, *representational* stage, more general invariants emerge – not just about *this* dog, but about dogs in general, say. These new structures impart to the child the great powers of symbolic functions, the most prominent of which is language. The invariants of all dogs can now be summarised and *re-presented* when they are not actually present, perhaps in the form of a drawing, or a word, or by a substitute object in play. Thus, with these new cognitive powers, the child enters an enormously creative and fascinating period of play.

And as these new powers themselves become co-ordinated, around seven years, so new, *concrete operational* structures are constructed which impart further cognitive powers, now of logical operations. Finally, these in turn become co-ordinated in early adolescence to form the structures of *formal operations*. Now the child has the powers to perform 'operations on operations', detached from specific materials or concrete situations, in a way which characterises scientific thinking.

In putting this constructivist view, Piaget was utterly scathing about associationism. It was a mistake, he said, to see development under the complete control of external connections (Piaget 1970). Instead, a stimulus is always filtered through an action–schema which in turn may be modified to produce novel adaptive responses. Piaget also minimised the role of prestructured innate factors. Maturation may have a limited role to play in the provision of the biological materials – which in turn provide the *possibilities* for the construction of cognitive structures. 'But this does not mean we can assume there exists a hereditary programme underlying the development of human intelligence: there are no "innate ideas" . . . Even logic is not innate, and only gives rise to a progressive epigenetic construction' (Piaget 1970, p. 720).

Piaget's theory has been criticised much of late, but most developmental psychologists still subscribe to the basic ideas (see papers in Richardson and Sheldon 1987). Although many 'Piagetians' are themselves revising the theory in some ways, the core philosophy of constructivism is adhered to intensely and faithfully (see papers in Shulman, Restaino-Baumann and Butler 1985; and Montangero 1985).

Bruner

Bruner's original theory (e.g. Bruner 1964) was based on the idea of three different kinds of mental representation, each involving different kinds of thinking – or 'technological advances in the use of the mind' (p. 1). These three modes of representation (modes of imposing organisation on sense data) are described as enactive ('represented in our muscles, so to speak' (p. 4), as with knowledge in bicycle riding, tying knots, etc.); iconic (broadly, the use of percepts and images) and symbolic (as in the use of arbitrary signs to stand for things, and in language). Development is a progressive acquisition of these three modes of representation, from the first to the last.

But the important point is that the *content* of these representation systems consists of 'amplifiers' – external implementation systems that extend our capacities. As described by Bruner (1966a) there are amplifiers of human motor capacities (tools and mechanical technologies); amplifiers of sensory capacities (from smoke-signals to radar); and amplifiers of human 'ratiocinative' capacities (theories, language, myth, explanation, etc.). Moreover, these amplifiers are, for the most part, 'conventionalised and transmitted in the culture' (p. 1). So that, in the course of acquiring the representation systems, and 'growing up', the child is really developing 'from the outside in'. This process is expedited by the fact that natural selection, in the course of evolution, has placed within us corresponding internal skills, which are 'represented genetically as capacities' (p. 2). Mentally, then, we come into the world biologically prepared for the acquisition of techniques which amplify our forms of representation.

In a landmark series of studies, which were in defiance of the behaviourist dogma of the time, and which helped trigger the 'cognitive revolution' in America, Bruner and his colleagues turned to 'thinking' and other central processes (Bruner, Goodnow and Austin 1956; Bruner 1966a). Many, if not most, of these were concerned with the transition from iconic to symbolic representation, and with demonstrating the benefits of the latter. For instance, in tasks in which a matrix of beakers varying in height and width has to be rearranged, 5-year-olds appeared to be dominated by immediate sensory experience and operate with one dimension at a time, whereas 7-year-olds were more 'rule-sensitive' and detached. (Again, the idea of a 'rule of synthesis' whereby variable objects are related to one another in a constructed representation.)

The immense amount of research that followed, however, has led to some change of emphasis in the different aspects of the theory. Thus, by the mid-1970s Bruner had abandoned his claim that 'mode of representation' is an adequate description of cognitive development and he no longer considers himself to be a stage theorist. Likewise, he came to emphasise language more as a means of access to intellectual tools evolved in the culture, and de-emphasised its role in thought *per se*. Along with this was an increasing interest in cultural transmission; the *structure* of the social context of this transmission thus came to be seen as the key to the mental structures that result. Accordingly, since the mid-1970s a major objective of Bruner's research has been to understand the structure of children's early social experience, and the connections between this and their language and their thought (see Bruner 1983).

Thus, the correspondence between sense experience, innate organising capabilities and representation (in thought and language) is identified by Bruner and his associates, not only in the first weeks of life, but also in the broader contexts of the structure of human social action and evolutionary history:

> there is a long evolutionary history that has shaped human immaturity and many of the elaborated forms of mother–infant interdependence are sufficiently invariant in our species to make inescapable the conclusion that they are in some crucial measure based on innate predispositions, however much these predispositions require priming by experience.
>
> (Bruner 1974, p. 263)

Many other child developmentalists would now go along with the idea that the richness of representation implicit in the social action of the child in, say, joint play and early language learning would be inconceivable without some innate organising base.

Vygotsky

This Soviet psychologist, who died at an early age in 1934, has recently become very popular in the West as a result of translations of his works published since the 1960s. These echo many of the ideas already described under Piaget and Bruner; but there are distinctions. First and foremost, Vygotsky traces his ideas to Karl Marx. 'I want to find out how science has to be built, to approach the study of the mind having learned the whole of Marx's method' (Vygotsky 1978, p. 8, quoted in Lee 1985, p. 67). But Marx's ideas derive from Kant, through Hegel, though in reaction to the idealistic elements of the latter.

> Men are the producers of their conceptions, ideas, etc. – real, active men, as they are conditioned by a definite development of their productive forces . . . Consciousness can never be anything else than conscious existence and the existence of men in their actual life process.
> (Marx 1959, p. 247, quoted in Lee 1985, p. 67)

Thus, conceptions, ideas, etc. derive from productive activities, not from pure thought, nor passive sense experience; but these productive activities take form in a social context, so there is a definite link between our concepts and ideas and the society in which we live.

With these foundations Vygotsky aimed for a unified, 'functional' psychology in which mental states were organised in relation to social action. In history, new forms of consciousness emerge when productive forces, and the social relations they imply, become reorganised on new levels. Development of the mind mimics this process in that it consists of spasmodic reorganisations, or revolutions, of consciousness. Moreover, the process involves incorporation of the outside social world to a large extent, especially in language, in which external social relations become captured in verbal thought:

> the very mechanism underlying higher mental functions is a copy from social interaction; all higher mental functions are internalised social relationships. These higher mental functions are the basis of the individual's social structure. Their composition, genetic [meaning developmental] structure, and means of action – in a word, their whole nature – is social. Even when we turn to mental processes, their nature remains quasi-social. In their own private sphere, human beings retain the functions of social interaction.
> (Vygotsky 1981, p. 161)

Thus, Vygotsky's constructivism rests on 'the aggregate of internalised social relations that have become functions for the individual and forms of his/her structure' (1981, p. 161). He was prepared to accept that development went through a stage in which the conditioned reflex or other simple associations played a part; but the intellectual functions which eventually emerge 'cannot be put in the same class as the mechanical formation of habits resulting from trial and error' (1981, p. 153). Likewise, there is an original innate core: 'Instinct, or the innate, inherited fund of behavioural modes' (1981, p. 153). But instead of having a continuing role in mentality, these relinquish their functions to the emerging intellectual functions.

> Cultural development is superimposed in the processes of growth, maturation, and the organic development of the child . . . The growth of the normal child into civilisation is usually a fusion with the processes of his/her organic maturation. Both planes of development – the natural and the cultural – coincide and mingle with one another. The two lines of changes interpenetrate and in essence form a single line of socio-biological formation of the child's personality.
> (Vygotsky 1960, p. 47, quoted in Lee 1985, p. 174)

Maps, models, plans, and so on

As mentioned in the previous chapter, associationists themselves had to concede, eventually, that there were some minor, constructive processes that were influential in learning and behaviour. It was Donald Hebb in the early post-war years who led the revolt against behaviourism: 'In mammals even as low as the rat', he declared, 'it has turned out to be impossible to describe behaviour as an interaction directly between sensory and motor processes . . . something like *thinking*, that is, intervenes' (Hebb 1949, p. XVI). And *thinking* could not be theorised very clearly in terms of mental associations. It required the construction of knowledge in a way in which gave rise to processes.

As also mentioned previously, the significance of central constructions was being realised well before Hebb. The running of rats in mazes played a significant part in this realisation (see Olton 1979 for a review). One of the mazes which Tolman, Ritchie and Kalsh (1946) used consisted of channels radiating in various directions, one of which led directly to food. Rats were first allowed access to food by a round-about route. When this route was blocked but a range of others made available, rats tended to choose the one that pointed most directly to the food. This behaviour could not be explained by simple S-R learning. Tolman described it as the construction of a *cognitive map*. Subsequent behaviourists tended to accept Tolman's view that conditioning involved knowledge in some shape or form, and tried to incorporate it into associationist theory, with limited success (Mackintosh 1983).

Hebb's conception of central processes was that of 'neural models' of the environment. Indeed, Craik (1943, p. 22) had already proposed that the nervous system is . . . a calculating machine capable of modelling or paralleling external events . . . If the organism carries a 'small scale model' of external reality and of its own possible actions within its head, it is able to try out various alternatives, conclude which is the best of them, react to future situations before they arise, utilise the knowledge of past events in dealing with the future, and in every way to react in a much fuller, safer and more competent manner to the emergencies which face it.

We have already seen how such ideas led eventually to the 'cognitive revolution'. We saw in the previous chapter how some of them were expressed in neo-associationist theories by the device of labelled relations working in tandem with some innate parsing processes. But the 'internal model' metaphor proliferated in other theories. One influential model was proposed by Miller, Galanter and Pribram (1960) in a book entitled *Plans and the Structure of Behaviour*. This was the TOTE (Test-Operate-Test-Exit) model, in which sensory input must be tested against central neural activity; the comparison initiates some operation which generates action either in some other part of the nervous system or (through behaviour) in the world. Mental imagery, too, has been seen as the manipulation of internal models (Pavio 1980; J.T.E. Richardson 1984). And the metaphor became popular among neuropsychologists, seeking to connect brain functions, behaviour and cognition. The aim is to show, as Pribram (1981, p. 154) put it, 'how the brain processes cognitions into perceptions and actions'. (He then adds: 'If this last statement sounds a little Kantian, it is meant to.')

Even at the level of functions of neurons in the cerebral cortex it is increasingly being claimed that 'top-down' processes, based on some kind of constructed model of the world, operate on incoming stimuli themselves (which are not, therefore, interpreted directly by 'bottom-up' analysis). Moreover, it is now quite generally accepted that these processes are likely to be based on the kind of parallel computations we discussed in the previous chapter, in which the streams of activity in different channels are being constantly shaped or 'gated' by each other, rather than being referred to some spatially fixed store or representation (Altman 1987).

Motor schema

It may by now be transpiring that a major theme in modern constructivism is that internal representations of the world are derived from *actions* in the world, and not merely from passive registration of associations in the environment. This is evident in the developmental theories of Piaget, Bruner and Vygotsky, and it is a theme which has also emerged in 'schema' theories of motor behaviour.

Whereas schemata were originally conceived as devices for explaining 'perceptual equivalence' – i.e. how the organism copes with environmental change and variability – in the motor domain we have the opposite problem. How do we account for the capacity, which all complex animals display, of generating an almost infinite variety of motor sequences to suit the particular demands of the moment? Hebb (1949) duly dubbed this capacity 'motor equivalence', and it is not difficult to illustrate. The skilled tennis player usually manages to return the ball to a small target area of court, even though the ball is received at different speeds, from different directions. The post-office parcels sorter always manages to hit the right bag from different initial positions with parcels of different weight, and so on (Pew 1974).

Such sheer variability and adaptability almost reach a scale on which no movement we make exactly replicates any *previous* movement we have made, and they are difficult to account for in terms of innate knowledge. They are also difficult to account for in terms of storage of specific motor programmes, each of which become associated with specific stimuli. The constant production of novel movements, quite apart from the problem of actually storing an almost infinite variety of motor programmes, makes this solution unlikely.

The suggestion that the notion of the schema may be applied to motor learning was first put in a paper by Pew (1974). The essence of this idea is that instead of a separate motor programme for each motor response, there are *generalised* motor programmes for each *class* of movement. Schmidt (1975) developed the suggestion into a major theory, which postulates, for instance, a single motor programme for the many ways of throwing a ball: 'These generalised programmes are assumed to be able to present the prestructured commands for a number of movements if specific response specifications are provided' (Schmidt 1975, p. 232). The idea helps account for many observations with which previous theories had difficulty (for instance, your signature written on a blackboard will almost certainly be similar to that written with pen and paper, even though quite different combinations of muscles and movements are used). And it has stood up well in preliminary experimental tests (e.g. Moxley 1979; and Shapiro and Schmidt 1982; see Kerr 1982 for useful discussion).

Object concepts

Object concepts have traditionally been at the centre of arguments between rationalists and associationists, and constructivism added a third solution to these two. You may remember that to rationalists, knowledge of a triangle, say, was, and still is, an innate idea, or pure concept, against which the degenerate (imperfect) forms of real experience are compared. To associationists, knowledge of a triangle is the abstracted set of common (associated) properties (three sides, three angles). Kant's solution was to propose 'rules of synthesis' by which experienced objects like triangles could be related to each other and so to the 'general conception' of triangle constructed from experience.

Of course, the idea of a 'rule of synthesis' sounds intuitively acceptable, but, scientifically, probably conceals far more than it reveals. None the less the idea has become prominent in theories of object concepts in the last two decades.

A concept is usually thought of as the mental representation of a category: either a 'natural' category such as *birds* or *furniture*, or an artificial category contrived out of two-dimensional geometric shapes or patterns. There have been some very active developments.

One development is the accumulation of evidence against the 'classical', associationistic view of concepts, in favour of a more 'probabilistic' view. The term 'schema' has only occasionally been used to describe this form of representation. An early use of the term in this context is that of Attneave (1957); and Evans (1967) described a schema as 'a characteristic of some population of objects, and consists of a set of *rules* serving as instructions for producing a population prototype (the concept)' (p. 87).

So that instead of a concept representing an object as either 'in' or 'out' of a particular category, according to rigid criteria (as the classical view insists), it is represented as belonging to this or that category with different degrees of *probability*.One empirical manifestation of this is that subjects will classify objects according to their relative probabilities of belonging in different categories: for example, a rabbit is classified among two categories, *mammal* and *fish*, much faster than is a whale. Among other manifestations are the so-called 'typicality effects'. In any given category some items or exemplars appear to be represented as more typical than others. For example, when subjects are asked to rate a list of birds for their typicality as birds, they will tend to rate robin higher than goose, sparrow higher than parrot, and so on, with a clear gradation among them (Rips, Shoben and Smith 1973). These effects cannot easily be explained by the classical view.

Thus, a concept now tends to be seen as some general representation, or schema, which is constructed from experience. In forming this construction the cognitive system is said to act 'creatively' on sense experience, with the creation of new higher-order information which was not directly available in experience (Mervis and Rosch 1981). A large number of models of concept formation have been developed in recent years, each attempting to describe the nature of construction and the higher-order information determining membership of exemplars (see Medin and Smith 1984; and Neisser 1987 for reviews). The construction of a category prototype – perhaps by averaging the experienced range of values in each feature of exemplars – is a very popular type of model. Another model suggests that the conceptual representation is simply the constructed record of the most frequently occurring features or feature values. There are many others. And each posits its peculiar set of 'rules' for membership determination: perhaps a way of calculating the 'distance' of a given exemplar from a category prototype; or a 'feature frequency sum', relevant to an assumed maximum.

Another important development has been the examination of the structural principles in the world itself which might determine category membership, and therefore the corresponding structure of the category concept. Rosch and her colleagues (e.g. Rosch *et al.* 1976; and Rosch and Mervis 1975) have suggested that we represent categories in the way that we do because of their intrinsic structure, in particular the relatedness among attributes as they occur in the category's exemplars. Attributes of birds, like beak and feathers, for instance, tend to occur together; so that attributes are not randomly occurring (e.g. beak and fur together are very rare). Moreover, we would expect this 'correlational structure' of categories in nature (in which there is a kind of 'family resemblance' among exemplars) to become reflected in our *concepts* of those categories: exemplars which share a lot of attributes with other exemplars would be expected to have high typicality, and to be classified relatively quickly, compared with exemplars whose attributes are shared by few other exemplars. Rosch and her colleagues have produced empirical evidence in support of this view (see references cited above).

It needs to be stressed that research in this area has given rise to many issues – including the one of whether any general representation needs to be posited at all to explain the research findings (see Medin and Smith 1984) – but it has been another area in which constructivist theory has been prominent in recent years.

Other schema theories

The notion of representation in the form of a schema has been broadened in recent years to describe more general representations of events and clusters of objects. The term itself is used more or less vaguely in this context. 'Like a concept, a schema is a representation abstracted from experience . . . A schema is a mental representation of a set of related categories' (Howard 1987, pp. 30–1). Sometimes the term 'frame' is used to indicate the representation of commonly recurring sets of objects and events in familiar contexts (e.g. Minsky 1975). Thus, we might possess the 'frame' of a home, the 'frame' of a school, and so on. Similarly, Schank and Abelson (1977) used the term 'script' to describe the representation of sequences of events following familiar general themes, in which particular details may vary. For example, we may have constructed a script for 'eating at a restaurant', another for 'getting dressed', and so on.

In each of these representations there are said to be sequences or clusters of

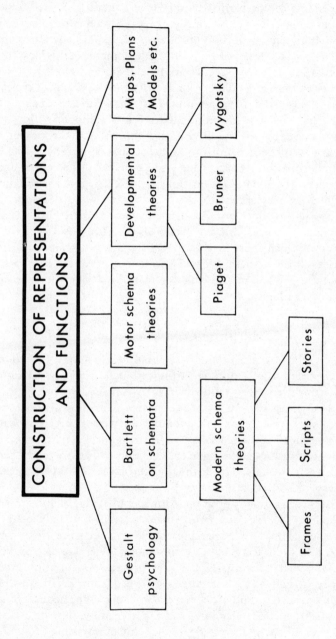

Figure 4.3 Some expressions of constructivism in contemporary theory

'slots', each 'slot' being filled by variable (though substitutable) events or objects, depending on the particular context (e.g. getting dressed for work versus getting dressed for a jog). Thus we might be said to possess a schema of the human body, in which concepts of arms, legs, and so on are organised in a particular way. There have been many developments of this idea, though these are often rather vague (see Thorndyke 1984; and Howard 1987 for useful reviews). One clearer illustration is that of Nelson and her colleagues (see Nelson 1986), who have attempted to show how ordinary object concepts develop out of script representations in childhood.

This is without doubt a very active area of theorising at the present time, and there have even been attempts to model schemata, scripts, and so on in terms of parallel distributed processing (see Rumelhart, McClelland and the PDP Research Group 1986). One possible promise that such theories hold is that of unifying a variety of constructivist theories, including developmental, and social theories (to which we will turn in the next chapter). But it remains to be seen whether such a promise will be realised. This must largely depend on the extent to which constructivist theories, generally, can overcome the many criticisms made of them. We will turn to these now, but for those who like a summary, a diagram showing the main branches of constructivist theory is shown in Figure 4.3.

Criticisms of constructivism

Perhaps we should look at criticisms by first reminding ourselves of the ways in which constructivism is different from rationalism and associationism. Constructivism differs from rationalism in two main respects. First, constructivist theories usually claim that mental representations are constructed in the course of experience in, and action on, the world; and constructed in such a way that these representations give rise to *functions* as part and parcel of the resulting structure. Second, these constructions take place on the basis of minimal innate constraints. The distinction in this second respect is usually, but not always, clear, so let us try to be explicit about it.

Rationalist theories usually posit pre-formed knowledge of quite considerable complexity – the rules of grammar of all possible human languages, or the major concepts of knowledge representation, for instance. Sense experience has a role only in 'triggering' or fine-tuning the emergence of these in development, which thus consists of a simple process of maturation. According to most constructivist theories there are, indeed, some innate constraints; but either these are very simple, and temporary, such as the neonate reflexes, which are quickly incorporated into, and superseded by, new mental structures; *or* they are of a very low grade, in the sense of imposing on sense data very basic distinctions. The logical distinctions operative in Kant's categories are the earliest example of this kind of innatism. Today, we are more likely to hear of the brain (or other information processes) constructing representations based only on the ability to distinguish between a few 'semantic primitives', such as feature components or other attributes of stimuli. But the basic principle is the same: innate knowledge and programmes that mature, or knowledge and programmes that are constructed when sense experience and action make contact with a few simple innate constraints. Thus, the issue is not whether something or nothing is innate (always remembering the difficulties with this idea, anyway, which we discussed in Chapter 2). As Cellerier (1980, p. 84) put it: 'no mental circuits will grow without genes to specify their anatomy, interconnection and physiology. The alternative thus becomes: is the mechanism a composer of programs or merely an executor?'

Of course, the distinction is not a perfect one. Whether we see the innate content as high-grade concepts and programmes, or low-grade discriminations, a continuum is implied. So that *some* authors who we might be inclined to view as rationalists might prefer to see themselves as constructivists, or vice versa. This difficulty is especially likely to arise in current cognitive psychology, where models of the mind having rationalist, associationist *and* constructivist elements are now proliferating at an enormous rate. These separate strands can be identified in the vast majority of cases, but occasionally there may be difficulties (often arising from vagueness in models themselves, rather than the inapplicability of the distinction we have been describing).

So what of the distinction between constructivism and associationism? Here again, the distinction is clear-cut in the vast majority of cases, but difficulties may be encountered. The clear-cut cases are those where constructivism is compared with 'classical' associationism or with S-R psychology. The comparison is between constructed representations and simple 'copies' of the world, and between constructed (and frequently novel) motor programmes and 'habits'. The difficulties arise with some 'neo-associationistic' theories that have emerged in the last two decades. Here we sometimes find mental associations as such confined to a restricted role such as memory storage, whilst other mental representations and functions are given a rationalist or constructivist basis. The trend appears to have terminated in full-blown constructivism in some 'information-processing' models based on simple 'wired-in' discriminations, in which structure clearly arises out of simple associations (see Papert 1980); and also in parallel distributed processing models where there is an 'innate' pattern of connections among processing units, but these are so modifiable as to allow the construction, effectively, of internal representations or schemata: 'the benefits of both nativism and empiricism' (Rumelhart, McClelland and the PDP Research Group 1986, p. 140). Generally speaking, though, we could say that constructivist theories abstract far more from sense experience than mere associations (e.g. rules, models, predictions, etc.).

This brings us, at last, to consider the criticisms of constructivism. By far the most general criticism is that constructivist theories tend to be rather vague. This has been a problem since Kant himself, who was notably obscure about key aspects; and the same applies to those who have followed in his tracks. What exactly *is* innate? What does it *do* to sense data? What is the *nature* of the schema which results? Whichever constructivist theories we look at, we find problems of this kind.

As a contemporary example we can look at Piaget's theory. Many who acknowledge the 'richness' of the theory also complain that the logical structures are abstract and difficult to operationalise (e.g. Case 1985). In the last twenty years many efforts have been made to overcome these problems by rendering Piaget's theory in information-processing terms – in other words, in terms of stored data and sequential processing steps, like a computer program (e.g. Pascual-Leone 1970; Case 1985; see Oakhill 1987 for review). But these have involved the introduction of further rationalist presuppositions. Thus, Case (1985) speaks of the child 'endowed with certain natural desires' (p. 59) and born with a 'basic repertoire of voluntary action schemes' (p. 93). Also, mental development, according to these theories, tends to be constrained, not by the stage of construction of mental structures themselves, but by the rate of growth of mechanical aspects of the system such as attentional resources (Pascual-Leone) or effective working memory space (Case). It remains to be seen whether theories like this really are more comprehensible and convincingly testable than the original.

Across the gamut of constructivist theories from Gestalt theory to modern 'schema' theories, there is the feeling that these are richer theories, but somehow difficult to grasp firmly. Remember that a good theory needs to specify, as precisely as possible, the components of the system, and their properties, and how these interrelate with one another, so that predictions and hypotheses can arise which can be empirically tested. A conspicuous feature of constructivist theorising in recent years has been the proliferation of imaginative models of knowledge formation and cognitive processing, all seeking internal consistency, but usually based on a minimum of theoretical constraints and many assumptions. The many kinds of computer modelling, including, more recently, the parallel processing models, are cases in point. But, as impressive as they are, *as* models, we have little evidence for their veracity. As Foss (1986, p. 95) says, such modelling 'leaves us with an impressive display of "connectionist" virtuosity but little reason to think that the skills displayed *are* embodied in grey matter'.

This brings us to consider the empirical evidence supporting constructivist theories. As with many associationist theories, there is an abundance of evidence in favour of specific constructivist theories; but this must not be accepted at face value. Piaget's theory again serves as a useful illustration. Over several decades, involving dozens, or even hundreds, of replications of investigations, Piaget and his co-workers produced evidence of, for example, their stage theory, and the presence or absence of certain logical structures at specific ages. But then researchers started to modify their procedures slightly, revealing abilities in children which were simply not brought out, or were inhibited, in the previous procedures, and the 'evidence' of Piaget started to crumble (see Donaldson 1978; and contributions in Richardson and Sheldon 1987). Moreover, studies in infancy, particularly around the subjects of communication and language development, have revealed *very early* mental complexity of a previously unsuspected degree (see contributions in Oates and Sheldon 1987). The equivocal nature of the evidence concerning other constructivist theories could also be mentioned.

All this brings us to the rather general point that it is really rather easy to obtain 'evidence' for a simplified (and sometimes vague) model of a complex system, especially when the model involves many untested assumptions. The usual procedure is to design an experiment; the model will predict the results; a 'fit' is found between the empirical results and the predicted results; so the model is taken as 'confirmed'. This is, scientifically, rather naïve. What we have to do with theories of complex systems (as many constructivist theories and refutations of theories have warned us) is to constantly compare the 'fit' of a model (i.e. between the model and the empirical results) with the 'fit' that would be obtained if the (untested) assumptions in the model were varied. In other words, in testing a model we must ensure that the results will eliminate *alternative* models.

The ubiquity of this kind of problem in constructivist theorising can be illustrated in the area of concept formation. As mentioned previously, many models of how concepts are formed and used have been produced in recent years. Each of these has been 'confirmed' by experimental results, even though there are many deep-seated incompatibilities among them, as models. Eventually, of course, investigators realised that a wide variety of different models (constructivist or otherwise) actually made similar or identical predictions about what would happen in particular experiments (Hayes-Roth and Hayes-Roth 1977; Richardson and Bhavnani 1984). No wonder evidence for constructivist models was easy to come by. Now the imperative of eliminating alternative models in the course of confirming one's own is understood, even though it taxes the experimenter's ingenuity considerably more than previously (Medin and Smith 1984; Richardson 1987).

In the light of these difficulties with constructivist models it is hardly surprising that traditional rationalists and associationists have been highly critical of them. Chomsky, for example, remains unimpressed by theories like that of Piaget, and finds them hopeless in accounting for the real structure of concepts and language: 'The expectation that constructions of sensory-motor intelligence determine the character of a mental organ such as language seems to me to be hardly more plausible than a proposal that the fundamental properties of the eye or the visual context or the heart develop on that basis' (1980, p. 37). Fodor (1980) suggests that constructivist theories, which propose a progression of structures of increasing power, are illogical, because they imply the emergence of a richer logic from a weaker one, which is impossible (for example, how does the weaker conceptual level, giving rise to a proposition at the richer level, 'know' that the proposition is valid?). Fodor thus declares: 'there literally isn't such a thing as the notion of learning a conceptual system richer than the one that one already has' (1980, p. 148).

Skinner finds constructivist theories not only wrong, but seriously misleading. Terms like 'intelligence', 'mental operations', 'reasoning', 'induction', 'thinking', 'imagery', and so on, are used without definition, he claims, and so cognitive scientists are accused 'of relaxing standards of definition and logical thinking and releasing a flood of speculation characteristic of metaphysics, literature, and daily intercourse . . . but inimicable to science' (1985, p. 300). The result of all this activity is that cognitive science offers *promises* of great achievements which have yet to be fulfilled (Skinner 1984).

Other criticisms strike more directly at some of the most fundamental assumptions of constructivism. Again, some of these have been brought together in the volume by Costall and Still (1987). Thus, Dreyfus and Dreyfus (1987) reiterate how much of constructivism, and of cognitive psychology generally, is based on the idea of mental 'rules'. But, in reality, these rules prove to be very elusive. For instance, experts in a particular knowledge domain (such as engineering, medicine or even chess) find it impossible actually to specify the rules that are supposed to provide the basis of their expertise. Other authors invoke the powerful views of J.J. Gibson (e.g. 1979), an investigator of perception, who argued that constructed representations in the brain are as unnecessary as either associations or innate interpretive powers. Instead, we perceive objects 'directly' by grasping the information they contain for some use. As Reed (1987, p. 97) explains: 'when we say "that banana looks good to eat" we are not speaking figuratively, but literally; nor are we simply "associating" a visual with a taste quality, we are simply seeing the fact of ripeness and edibility'.

Criticisms of this kind do not necessarily mean that constructivism is fatally flawed. One reason why such theories are indeed vulnerable to such attacks is precisely that they have been prepared to tackle 'big' questions in a way which at least acknowledges the complexity of the system. If we are unhappy about burying this complexity out of sight in the innate concepts and processes of rationalism, or about reducing it to simple associations, then we face a phenomenally difficult task. Continued criticism will be crucial in wringing genuine progress out of this confrontation.

Finally, we have to remember that an adequate theory of psychology needs to be a theory of the 'whole' mental system – feelings and appetites, as well as cognitions. In associationism from Aristotle to Thorndike, the Law of Effect clearly tied these together. The struggle between rational reason, and irrational appetites and feelings, in rationalist theory, has been an equally long story. Kant similarly viewed all motives as essentially irrational, and in need of the careful control of reason and moral law. Around this perceived need he constructed a wide-ranging theory of ethics. Constructivism in the twentieth century, however, has tended to be one-sided. Bartlett (1932) linked remembering with personal feelings and social conventions, and Piaget (1932) attempted to describe moral development, but the more recent constructivists have tended to focus on principles of cognition as an independent system. Even motivation has been treated as a force intrinsic to that system alone – an intrinsic drive for harmonious construction itself. For example, Hunt (1971) has described motivation as an automatic response to *incongruity* between existing cognitive structures and present experience. This is reminiscent of the effects of loss of equilibration (between assimilation and accommodation), as described by Piaget. Bruner (1966b) saw curiosity as the main expression of this intrinsic force: 'Almost all children possess what have come to be called "intrinsic" motives for learning. An intrinsic motive is one that does not depend upon reward that lies outside the activity it impels. Reward inheres in the successful termination of the activity or even in the activity itself' (pp. 132–3). There have been many criticisms of this one-sidedness of recent, 'cognitive' constructivism, and we will turn to some of these in the next chapter.

References

Altman, J. (1987) A quiet revolution in thinking. *Nature*, 328, 572–3.

Arnheim, R. (1986) The two faces of Gestalt psychology. *American Psychologist*, 41, 820–4.

Attneave, F. (1957) Transfer of experience with a class-schema to identification learning of patterns and shapes. *Journal of Experimental Psychology*, 54, 81–8.

Bartlett, F.C. (1932) *Remembering: A Study in Experimental and Social Psychology*. Cambridge, Cambridge University Press.

Bartlett, F.C. (1958) *Thinking: An Experimental and Social Study*. London, Allen & Unwin.

Bruner, J.S. (1964) The course of cognitive growth. *American Psychologist*, 15, 1–15.

Bruner, J.S. (1966a) On cognitive growth. In J.S. Bruner, R.R. Olver and P. Greenfield (eds.), *Studies in Cognitive Growth*. New York, Wiley.

Bruner, J.S. (1966b) *Towards a Theory of Instruction*. New York, Norton.

Bruner, J.S. (1974) From communication to language – a psychological perspective. *Cognition*, 3, 255–78.

Bruner, J.S. (1983) *In Search of Mind*. New York, Harper & Row.

Bruner, J.S., Goodnow, J.J. and Austin, G.A. (1956) *A Study of Thinking*. New York, Wiley.

Case, R. (1985) *Intellectual Development: Birth to Adulthood.* New York, Academic Press.

Cellerier, G. (1980) Some clarifications on innatism and constructivism. In M. Piattelli-Palmarini (ed.), *Language and Learning: The Debate between Jean Piaget and Noam Chomsky.* London, Routledge & Kegan Paul.

Chomsky, N. (1980). On cognitive structures and their development: a reply to Piaget. In M. Piattelli-Palmarini (ed.), *Language and Learning: The Debate between Jean Piaget and Noam Chomsky.* London, Routledge & Kegan Paul.

Costall, A. and Still, A. (1987) *Cognitive Psychology in Question.* New York, St Martin's Press.

Craik, K. (1943) *The Nature of Explanation.* Cambridge, Cambridge University Press.

Donaldson, M. (1978) *Children's Minds.* London, Fontana.

Dreyfus, H.L. and Dreyfus, S.E. (1987) The mistaken psychological assumptions underlying the belief in expert systems. In A. Costall and A. Still (eds.), *Cognitive Psychology in Question.* New York, St Martin's Press.

Edwards, D. and Middleton, D. (1987) Conversation and remembering: Bartlett revisited. *Applied Cognitive Psychology,* 1, 77–92.

Evans, S.H. (1967) A brief statement of schema theory. *Psychonomic Science,* 8, 87–8.

Fodor, J. (1980) Fixation of belief and concept acquisition. In M. Piattelli-Palmarini (ed.), *Language and Learning: The Debate between Jean Piaget and Noam Chomsky.* London, Routledge & Kegan Paul.

Foss, J. (1986) Abstract solutions versus neurobiologically plausible problems. *The Behavioral and Brain Sciences,* 9, 95–6.

Gibson, J.J. (1979) *The Ecological Approach to Visual Perception.* Boston, Houghton-Mifflin.

Hayes-Roth, B. and Hayes-Roth, F. (1977) Concept learning and the recognition and classification of exemplars. *Journal of Verbal Learning and Verbal Behavior,* 16, 119–36.

Hebb, D.O. (1949) *The Organisation of Behaviour.* New York, Wiley.

Howard, R.W. (1987) *Concepts and Schemata: An Introduction.* London, Cassell.

Hunt, J. McV. (1971) Using intrinsic motivation to teach young children. *Education Technology,* 2, 78–80.

Kaufman, W. (1980) *Discovering the Mind,* Vol. 1: *Goethe, Kant and Hegel.* New York, McGraw-Hill.

Kerr, R. (1982) *Psychomotor Learning.* New York, Saunders College Publishing.

Lee, B. (1985) Intellectual origins of Vygotsky's semiotic analysis. In J.V. Wertsch (ed.), *Culture Communication and Cognition: Vygotskyan Perspectives.* Cambridge, Cambridge University Press.

Mackintosh, N.J. (1983) *Conditioning and Associative Learning.* Oxford, Clarendon Press.

Marx, K. (1959) *Marx and Engels: Basic Writings in Politics and Philosophy,* (ed.) L.S. Feuer, New York, Doubleday.

Medin, D.L. and Smith, E.E. (1984) Concepts and concept formation. *Annual Review of Psychology,* 91, 289–316.

Mervis, C.B. and Rosch, E. (1981) Categorisation of natural objects. *Annual Review of Psychology,* 32, 89–115.

Miller, G.A., Galanter, E. and Pribram, K. (1960) *Plans and the Structure of Action*. New York, Holt.

Minsky, M. (1975) A framework for representing knowledge. In P.H. Winston (ed.), *The Psychology of Computer Vision*. New York, McGraw-Hill.

Montangero, J. (1985) *Genetic Epistemology: Yesterday and Today*. New York, Graduate School and University Center, City University of New York.

Moxley, S.E. (1979) Schema: the variability of practice hypothesis. *Journal of Motor Behaviour*, 11, 65–70.

Neisser, U. (ed.) (1987) *Concepts and Conceptual Development*. Cambridge, Cambridge University Press.

Nelson, K. (ed.) (1986) *Event Knowledge: Structure and Function in Development*. Hillsdale, Lawrence Erlbaum.

Oakhill, J. (1987) The development of children's reasoning ability: information-processing approaches. In K. Richardson and S. Sheldon (eds.), *Cognitive Development to Adolescence*. Hove, Lawrence Erlbaum.

Oates, J. and Sheldon, S. (eds.) (1987) *Cognitive Development in Infancy*. Hove. Lawrence Erlbaum.

Olton, D.S. (ed.) (1979) Mazes, maps and memory. *American Psychologist*, 34, 583–96.

Papert, S. (1980) The role of artificial intelligence in psychology. In M. Piattelli-Palmarini (ed.), *Language and Learning: The Debate between Jean Piaget and Noam Chomsky*. London, Routledge & Kegan Paul.

Pascual-Leone, J. (1970) A mathematical model for the transition rule in Piaget's developmental stages. *Acta Psychologia*, 32, 301–45.

Pavio, A. (1986) *Mental Representation: a Dual Coding Approach*. Oxford, Oxford University Press.

Pew, R.W. (1974) Human perceptual-motor performance. In B.H. Kantowitz (ed.), *Human Information Processing: Tutorials in Performance and Cognition*. New York, Lawrence Erlbaum.

Piaget, J. (1932) *The Moral Development of the Child*. London, Routledge & Kegan Paul.

Piaget, J. (1970) Piaget's theory. In P.H. Mussen (ed.), *Manual of Child Psychology*. London, Wiley.

Pribram, K.H. (1981) The brain as the locus of controls on action. In G. d'Ydewalle and W. Lens (eds.) *Cognition in Human Motivation and Learning*. Leuven and Hillsdale, New Jersey, Leuven University Press and Erlbaum.

Reed, E. (1987) Why do things look as they do? The implications of James Gibson's *The ecological approach to visual perception*. In A. Costall and A. Still (eds.), *Cognitive Psychology in Question*. New York, St Martin's Press.

Richardson, J.T.E. (1980) *Mental Imagery and Human Memory*. London, Macmillan.

Richardson, K. and Bhavnani, K.K. (1984) How a concept is formed: prototype or contingency abstraction? *British Journal of Psychology*, 75, 507–19.

Richardson, K. and Sheldon, S. (eds.) (1987) *Cognitive Development to Adolescence*. Hove, Lawrence Erlbaum.

Rips, L.J., Shoben, E.J. and Smith, E.E. (1973) Semantic distance and the verification of semantic relations. *Journal of Verbal Learning and Verbal Behavior*, 23, 1–20.

Robinson, D.N. (1981) *An Intellectual History of Psychology*. New York, Macmillan.

Rosch, E. and Mervis, C. (1975) Family resemblances: studies in the internal structure of categories. *Cognitive Psychology*, 7, 573–605.

Rosch, E., Mervis, C.B., Gray, W., Johnson, D. and Boyes-Braem, P. (1976) Basic objects in material categories. *Cognitive Psychology*, 8, 382–439.

Rumelhart, D.E., McClelland, J.L. and the PDP Research Group (1986) *Parallel Distributed Processing: Explorations in the Microstructure of Cognition*, Vol. 1, *Foundations*. Cambridge, Mass., MIT Press.

Schanks, R.C. and Abelson, R.P. (1977) *Scripts, Plans, Goals and Understanding.* Hillsdale, Lawrence Erlbaum.

Schmidt, R.A. (1975) A schema theory of discrete motor skill learning. *Psychological Review*, 82, 225–60.

Schroder, G. (1968) Kant's theory of concepts. In R.P. Wolff (ed.), *Kant: A Collection of Critical Essays*. London, Macmillan.

Shapiro, D.C. and Schmidt, R.A. (1982) The schema theory: recent evidence and developmental implications. In J.A.S. Kelso and J.E. Clarke (eds.), *The Development of Movement Control and Coordination*. New York, Wiley.

Shulman, V.L., Restaino-Baumann, L.C.R. and Butler, L. (eds.) (1985), *The Future of Piagetian Theory: The Neo-Piagetians*. New York, Plenum Press.

Skinner, B.F. (1984) Responses. *The Behavioral and Brain Sciences*, 7, 507.

Skinner, B.F. (1985) Cognitive science and behaviourism. *British Journal of Psychology*, 76, 291–301.

Thorndyke, P.W. (1984) Applications of schema theory in cognitive research. In J.R. Anderson and S.M. Kosslyn (eds.), *Tutorials in Learning and Memory*. San Francisco, W.H. Freeman.

Tolman, E.C., Ritchie, E.B. and Kalsh, D. (1946) Studies in spatial learning 1: orientation and the short cut. *Journal of Experimental Psychology*, 36, 13–24.

Vygotsky, L.S. (1978) *Mind in Society*, (ed.) M. Cole, V. John-Steiner, S. Scribner and E. Souberman. Cambridge, Mass., Harvard University Press.

Vygotsky, L.S. (1981) The genesis of higher mental functions. In J. Wertsch (ed.), *The Concept of Activity in Soviet Psychology*. Armonck, Sharpe.

Walsh, W.H. (1968) Schematism. In R.P. Wolff (ed.), *Kant: A Collection of Critical Essays*. London, Macmillan.

Wolff, R.P. (ed.) (1968) *Kant: A Collection of Critical Essays*. London, Macmillan.

5

The Individual and the Social

Another important theme in psychology, which cuts right across all the others mentioned so far, is the relation between the individual and the social. As with the other themes, this one reflects opposing sets of presuppositions – this time about which set of determinants of human knowledge and behaviour have priority, those arising from within the individual or those arising from the network of human relations to which, as human beings, we all belong. Although these presuppositions have counterposed each other from antiquity (see Dumont 1965), since the seventeenth century psychological theory has definitely been dominated by the idea of the autonomous individual as the source of knowledge and conduct.

The rise of modern science in the seventeenth century, and with it the modern conception of the individual in economics, politics and psychology, was in fact the culmination of widespread social and economic changes that, at least partly, formed the basis of that conception. With the breakdown of feudalism over the previous two centuries, and with it the dissolution of relations of mutual obligation among people, the latter became 'free' in a double sense: free of all rights to land and property that had formerly been theirs; and free of the corporate relations that had gone with them. In this sense, all over Europe, societies became composed of individuals whose only means of life was the sale of their individual labour power, and who had never been individuals in that sense before.

It is difficult for us to grasp, today, living in a world now used to such individualism, the great import of these changes, and what they have meant for psychology ever since. But many have commented on the new conception of human nature which emerged. For example, in Shakespeare's *King Lear*, Marshall McLuhan finds a critical appraisal of how 'The new patterns of power and organisation which had been discussed during the preceding century were now, in the early seventeeth century, being felt at all levels of social and private life', and how 'Competitive individualism had become the scandal of a society long invested with corporate and collective values'

(McLuhan 1962, pp. 11, 12). And among philosophers, few have stressed the disjunction which emerged between individual and society more strongly than Karl Marx:

> In this society of free competition, the individual appears detached from natural bonds, etc. which in earlier historical periods make him the accessory of a definite and limited human conglomerate . . . The more deeply we go back in history, the more does the individual, and hence also the producing individual, appear as dependent, as belonging to a greater whole . . . Only in the eighteenth century, in 'civil society', do the various forms of social connectedness confront the individual as a mere means towards his private purposes.
>
> (Marx 1973, pp. 83–4)

It is possible to imagine the difficulty faced by the 'new wave' of philosophers in the seventeenth century who were trying to theorise about the mind in the context of this emerging individualism. Others have noted how the problem for Descartes and his generation was that of putting soul and body back together in a rather special way, 'a way as to stand in need of nothing beyond themselves individually' (Whitehead 1928, p. 179). It is well known how Descartes conceived of the mind, with its innate ideas, lodged in a quasi-mechanical body. Thus, he bequeathed us the encapsulated mind, the embodied self. As Bertrand Russell (1962, p. 125) put it, in Descartes 'everyone is thrown back on his personal existence as a basis for knowledge'.

Through Hobbes (to whom the human life was 'solitary, poor, nasty, brutish and short', and who saw society merely as a device, a necessity, for curtailing the 'war of all against all'), and Locke, Hume and the other philosopher-psychologists of the eighteenth and nineteenth centuries, the presupposition of the detached individual, learning, thinking and behaving in the interests of the self, came to pervade modern psychology up to the present day. But it has created a perennial problem. Since society obviously exists, what is the relation between the psychological individual and society? In this chapter, then, we shall illustrate the ways in which various psychologists have theorised about this problem, from those who have tried to 'explain' and reconcile the disjunction, to those who have claimed that the disjunction, in reality, does not exist. We shall follow the framework used so far in this book, remembering, as before, that it is a simplification which, although useful, should not be taken as perfectly exact.

Social rationalism

Like rationalist theories generally, *social* rationalist theories are based on the presupposition of innate social knowledge, drives, motives, and so on, within the individual. The herd instinct, long attributed to animals which congregate, became attributed to humans, too, by William McDougall (*An Introduction to Social Psychology*, 1968). This book was reprinted many times, until its last edition in 1935, and became standard reading for generations of psychology students. As with instincts in general (see Chapter 2) it became fashionable to 'explain' all manner of conventionalised social behaviours by calling them instincts. McDougall even proposed the existence of a kind of nationalistic instinct – an innate identity with country, nationalist symbols, 'race', etc.

Since the mid-1930s, however, new varieties of instinct theory have been proposed by behavioural biologists. These were largely prompted by the ethological field studies of Niko Tinbergen and Konrad Lorenz, which were also mentioned in Chapter 2. They have had a powerful impact in psychology. Most of the sign stimuli discussed by the ethologists are social, in the sense of evoking or inhibiting fixed routines in others of the same species. Thus, they are often called communicative behaviours. For instance, Lorenz has shown that in cyclid fishes, some birds and one or two other species, 'aggressive' displays keep rivals away from a breeding or feeding territory, thereby achieving a balanced dispersal of the species and a minimum of nutritional competition. Lorenz argues that such instincts, laid down in our phylogenetic ancestors, are still 'inside' us. 'Human behaviour, and particularly human social behaviour . . . is still subject to all the laws prevailing in all phylogenetically adapted human behaviour. Of these laws, we possess a fair amount of knowledge from studying the instincts of animals' (Lorenz 1966, p. 204).

Like McDougall, Lorenz also proposes an instinct of group identification: 'The urge to embrace some sort of cause, to pledge allegiance to some sort of ideal, in short to *belong* to some sort of human group, is as strong as that of any other instinct' (in Evans 1975, p. 251). Following Lorenz's *On Aggression*, a number of other polemical texts claimed a biological basis for what they saw as universal social traits. These included Ardrey (1968) on our alleged *territoriality*; Tiger and Fox (1971), telling us that 'we remain Upper Paleolithic hunters . . . [having] deeper primate motives devoted to the pursuit of unfair shares and an unequal access to control over genes [i.e. mates] and privilege' (pp. 21, 25); and Morris (1967) on our crude sexuality.

More recently, this kind of theorising has emerged in the guise of a 'new synthesis' called *sociobiology* (Wilson 1975). Based on certain genetic hypotheses concerning the behaviour of social insects such as bees and ants, the upshot of this synthesis is that there are inescapable genetic constraints on human social behaviour which unconsciously shape and channel our social interactions. Take, for example, the behavioural tendencies of men and women:

Some of the traditional differences between men and women, such as their novelty drive, the active versus receptive nature of their libidos and the speed of their sexual response cycles, are fundamentally built into their biology, and society is bound to accommodate them. It is no good pretending that they do not exist.

(Wilson 1979, p. 353)

In such ways our biologies are said to shape not just our individual behaviours towards others, but also our social structures, which thus tend to be fixed, at least in many respects. Also, so it is argued, forms of perception which influence social behaviours, and such aspects of culture as tools, taboos, food items, dreams, conventions, art and even scientific theories, are related to genotypes, and vary across cultures, to some extent, because the genotypes vary (Lumsden and Wilson 1981). A rather extreme argument is that because people within cultural groups share more genes (so it is assumed) they identify with each other more than people between groups, and this disposes people to express a kind of 'race hatred' to others outside their group; thus, according to Barash (1979, p. 153), there may be 'an evolutionary tendency to racism'.

These illustrate rationalist theories of social effects which are believed to prevail throughout life in the individual and across many generations in the society. There are other theories, however, which are more concerned with the child 'becoming' social, and being able to enter into social interactions in the first place. Best known of these, perhaps, is John Bowlby's claim that every infant has a need and a biological predisposition to 'bond' with one particular adult, usually the mother (e.g. Bowlby 1969). Failure to experience such bonding can have detrimental long-term effects. The mechanisms of the bonding are unclear in most theories, but some sort of innate signalling system is often thought to be involved. Studies of bonding across widely different cultures are taken to offer support for these theories (see, for example, Eibl-Eibesfeldt 1983).

One important way in which infants and children develop skills and behaviour patterns that are part of their culture is through imitation. Meltzoff and his associates (e.g. Meltzoff and Moore 1983) have claimed, on the basis of observing very young infants' imitations of parents' facial gestures, that it is an 'apparently innate proclivity' (p. 297). Somewhat similarly, Trevarthen (1983) argues that the cognitive skills required (and observed) in infant–parent interactions are of such complexity that we must conclude 'that innate interpersonal abilities regulate and drive forward the growth of co-operative awareness' (p. 145). Bruner, too (e.g. 1981), whom we would generally think of as a constructivist, has argued, like Chomsky, that early communication and language acquisition are assisted by an innate language acquisition device (LAD), but supported by a language acquisition service (LAS) in the adult. Generally speaking, rationalist (or neo-rationalist) theories of social abilities have become increasingly popular in the last few years.

Criticisms of social rationalism are similar to those of rationalism generally. First, allusions to the innate tend to emerge when psychologists find themselves unable to explain a phenomenon in any other way. Issues tend, as it were, to become 'dumped' in this way. Once entertained, or even accepted, some quite wild conclusions are then occasionally drawn. Plausible stories are then taken as empirical fact, when no theory has actually been empirically tested.

Difficulties of testing such theories arise, first, because the theories themselves tend to be exceptionally sketchy. It is one thing to say that a particular social proclivity is innate, but quite another to turn that statement into a theory – a 'model' of what is innate – which can generate predictions that can, in turn, be empirically tested. Moreover, nothing is really explained by calling it innate. Even if it is innate, we still have to explain *why* and *how* it is innate – for example, by some non-trivial and generally acceptable evolutionary or selection argument (these themselves are often fraught with uncertainty or oversimplification, as we saw in Chapter 2). And we still have to remember that 'innate' does not mean unchangeable. Instead of constructing clear theory, social rationalists, like rationalists generally, tend to argue loosely by analogy with simpler skills or with simpler species. This is particularly the case with sociobiology. Recently, Kitcher (1985; 1987) has completed a thorough critique of this style of argument in what he calls 'pop sociobiology' (to distinguish it from the more cautious varieties). Beckwith (1987, p. 72) lists these 'numerous transgressions of normal scientific method' as

> lack of sufficient data, invoking confounding variables when they are needed and ignoring them in other cases, misreporting of the 'findings of students of animal behaviour', failure to consider alternative competing explanations, mystification by use of inapplicable mathematical formulations, misuse of anthropomorphic language in comparing the behaviour of humans and other animals, and a host more.

Social associationism

Associationists who have considered the social context of human existence have treated society as an environment not fundamentally different, for analytical purposes, from any other. Social responses are just individual responses like any other responses, and the gestures and responses of other people are just stimuli and/or reinforcers, like any others. Social behaviour is still motivated by individualistic drives, appetites, and so on.

Although the earlier British associationists speculated about the laws of association in a social context – e.g. in forming 'good habits' in school and in society generally – most social associationist theory this century has been in the behaviourist framework. Not surprisingly this has relied to a large extent on the notion of secondary reinforcement, simply because it soon occurred, even to the staunchest behaviourists, that there are few human behaviours that are directly reinforced by primary reinforcers such as food, drink, release from punishment, and so on. As described in Chapter 3, an event that is frequently associated with a primary reinforcer in nature can acquire the powers of a secondary reinforcer in relation to the respondent or operant behaviour, and thus elicit or determine behaviours in rather the same way. As Racklin (1970, p. 123) explains:

> Secondary reinforcement bridges the gap between laboratory proce-
> dures and complex human and animal behaviour . . . A newborn
> baby's rewards are easy to enumerate: milk, a change of diapers and a
> certain amount of fondling by its parents. As the baby grows up, the list
> of things that he will work to produce may be enlarged to include
> praise, money, fame, achievement, and so forth. A dollar bill may not
> be as rewarding to a baby as a shiny dime. As he grows older, though,
> the dirty green piece of paper may become relatively sought after. It is
> reasonable to explain this change as a case of secondary reinforcement –
> the dollar has become linked to other reinforcements.

Skinner likewise generalises from reinforcement to social reinforcement. The good society is one in which secondary reinforcers are identified, and contingencies of reinforcement are arranged for the benefit of all.

> Food, sex, music and all other values are reinforcers . . . We must
> arrange effective contingencies of reinforcement. In doing so we
> supplement the economic sanctions of Adam Smith. In doing so we can
> do better than the Utopian reformers and move closer to a world in
> which we can be productive and happy.
>
>   (Skinner 1972, p. 136)

Skinner even wrote a novel, *Walden II*, about a model society organised along these lines. In this society, as in Skinner's theory generally, 'good' social behaviours are the results of harmonious and consistent contingencies of reinforcement. Antisocial behaviours are the result of inappropriate, or inconsistent, contingencies of reinforcement. Either way, in our relations with other people, we are all unwitting behaviour shapers and become behaviourally shaped.

This view of social reinforcement as a mediator of material reinforcement has certainly been very popular (see Reykowski 1982). Thus, many pro-grammes of instruction in school, or of behaviour therapy for the correction of antisocial behaviours, have been devised, based on the contingent use of verbal praise, smiles, touching, and so on. Programmes of 'group contingencies' such as scores for a class in school have also been tried, to foster academic performance and reduce disruptive behaviour (e.g. Pigott, Fantuzzo and Clement 1986; Strain 1981). Bandura's (e.g. 1986) social learning theory has augmented these principles with others which stress the individual's self-reactive control and guidance of his or her own behaviour in a social context.

Criticisms of social associationism have tended to focus on the more sensationalistic aspects of what are seen as programmes of social engineering. 'Someone', it is argued, must have ultimate responsibility for arranging contingencies of social reinforcement: who controls *that* person? It is a question that seems fair. As Carpenter (1974) notes about operant principles in a human social context:

> In general, the socialisation of young people, that is, the shaping of their behaviour so that they can function effectively and constructively in social settings, is a kind of brainwashing process. But it is a brainwashing that is necessary for a surviving society, which needs the cohesion supplied by mutual reinforcement. There is no possible way that a person can be socialised without also being controlled by the people in his environment. The person is always easier to change than the whole social system. Hence, it is most convenient and practical to shape the child's behaviour so that it is reasonably compatible with that of his associates.
>
> (pp. 192–3)

If, in the terms of the examination question, you were presented with such a statement, and told to 'Discuss', you would soon realise that issues intertwined here are more than strictly psychological.

From a strictly psychological viewpoint, the criticisms of social associationism are similar to those of associationism generally. Most importantly, it assumes a static quality and permanence of things associated in the social world, just as they are assumed to be in the natural world. The criticism is that the social world is full of flux and change, so that only rarely are social phenomena repeatedly and consistently associated. A touch on the arm from a friend in, say, a bar might be associated with some material 'reinforcer' – but not the touch on the arm from the policeman as I get out of my car. The significance of the event varies from context to context, and may very well have significance even when the context is quite unique. As Chomsky complained about Skinner's account of that most social of behaviours, language – i.e. that it was acquired by a process of secondary reinforcement – some recourse to more abstract principles seems inescapable.

The other important criticism is, of course, that just because some social behaviour is amenable to analysis and explanation in behaviouristic terms, this does not necessarily mean that *all* social behaviour is *necessarily* best described in these terms. This is the old argument against reductionism that acquires still greater force when we are talking about humans behaving together as a society.

Social constructivism

Most – but not all – constructivism is *social* constructivism, to the extent that it is recognised that if we, indeed, construct models of the world in the course of our actions on it, the vast majority of our actions are actually done not individually but in co-operation with other human beings. Thus the mental models we construct are shared among our social networks in a very deep sense, and this sharing makes further co-operation easier and more efficient, and so on. Thus, in social constructivism, the difference between the individual and the social, as sources of knowledge, is largely dissolved. But this does not mean that individuals are reduced to an amorphous mass consciousness. On the contrary, many social constructivists argue that people become fulfilled, autonomous individuals only *by virtue* of their social actions – that humans 'individuate' only in the midst of society.

Jerome Bruner is perhaps the best known of contemporary social constructivists. In his early theorising (e.g. Bruner 1964) human cognitive development is portrayed as the acquisition of social-technical skills, 'from the outside in'. He quotes the work of anthropologists (e.g. Washburn and Howell 1960) which suggests the importance of a social way of life, tool-making, and so on, as *antecedents* of the evolution of large brain size. This means that most of our present cerebral-cognitive apparatus has been substantially fashioned *by* the requirements of such a way of life. For instance, the demands on our cognitive apparatus of anticipating the perceptions of *other* humans, and of programming our own actions to mix harmoniously with *their* actions, are infinitely greater than the (already great) demands of individual confrontation with the world. The fact that our brains are – even in relative terms – three times bigger than those of our nearest biological cousins (chimpanzees) is likely to have something to do with such demands.

The more recent fossil evidence has reinforced this view, as Holloway (1975) has pointed. So we are left with a view of the relation between individual and society, in which 'Like the cabbage it so much resembles, the homo sapiens brain, having arisen within the framework of human culture, would not be viable outside of it' (Geertz 1962, p. 724).

Culture, in the sense of forms of production, tools and machines, social conventions, symbols, music, dance, and so on, is the outermost, tangible expression of those shared models of reality. The recognition of this explains the close affinity between many social constructivists and cultural anthropologists. Vygotsky, indeed, spoke of child cognitive development as *cultural* development. The deeply social nature of his theory, and of its relation with cultural forms, such as material production, was described in the previous chapter. According to this theory, the fundamental motor of development is the recurrence of 'clashes' between the child's constructed model of reality, and that implicitly shared in the social group to which the child belongs. 'The very essence of cultural development is in the collision of mature cultural forms of behaviour with the primitive forms that characterise the child's behaviour' (Vygotsky, in Wertsch 1981, p. 149).

But the recognition of the connection between individual knowledge and external culture has led to recent investigations of the role of culture in early development in Britain and the USA as well. Cultural transmission, especially through the medium of language, and other forms of communication in infancy, became a major focus of Bruner's research, for instance. The structure of the social context of this transmission came to be seen as the key to the understanding of the mental structures that result. Accordingly, since the mid-1970s a major objective of research has been to understand the structure of children's early social experience, and the connections between this and their language and their thought (see Bruner 1983).

Piaget remains something of an oddity when social aspects of his constructivism are considered. Although some of his earlier works, such as *The Moral Judgement of the Child*, published in 1932, stressed the importance of social interaction, such expressions became increasingly sporadic as Piaget became preoccupied with the logical structures in the abstract (epistemic) individual. Indeed, Piaget's theory has been subjected to increasing criticism over the last few years because of its 'unsocial' nature (e.g. Donaldson 1978; Light 1983).

A number of Piaget's successors, however, have augmented the theory to include social considerations, and both this broader theory and the research which has followed have been very influential (see, for example, Perret-Clermont 1980; Doise and Mugny 1984). As Doise (1985, p. 102) explains, in Piaget's writings 'the social is involved as an explicative factor but without being demonstrated in the proper sense'. Accordingly, the research of Doise and his colleagues in Geneva and Neuchâtel set out to illustrate how social interactions can foster the emergence of certain cognitive operations. For example, children who, on pre-tests with certain Piagetian tasks, were found to be 'pre-operational' (i.e. had not yet reached the stage of concrete operations, which includes the ability to predict and reverse transformations in more than one dimension at a time) were allowed to co-operate in pairs in tackling further tasks. The act of co-operation led to appreciable gains in the post-test, as if the confrontation with another 'point of view' had led to rapid 'cognitive restructuration' (Doise 1985). The new appreciation that has emerged, of the testing situation – and indeed any instructional situation – as a *social* situation, is one fruitful product of this branch of social-constructivist theorising (e.g. Perret-Clermont and Bell 1987).

The convergence of various lines of this sort has recently resulted in a clearly defined sub-discipline called 'social cognition' (see e.g. contributions in Butterworth and Light 1981; and in Richards and Light 1987). As Ingleby (1987) put it: 'Looking a little closer, we see that a single idea unites recent thinking both *in* and *about* psychology; namely, the idea that "mind" is situated in practical activity, and cannot be understood outside of its social and historical context' (p. 298). Though the spread of the idea is almost certainly narrower than implied by Ingleby in the quote, social cognition – or cognition as a function of human social action – is now at the forefront of developmental psychology, at least.

These are all illustrations from developmental psychology, but much social constructivism can be found in social psychology generally. Much of this, in turn, stems from the work of George Herbert Mead (*Self and Society*, 1937), who saw joint action as the distinguishing feature of human society. Much of social interaction is itself based on an intricate kind of knowledge – of rights and obligations, roles and conventions, for example – that is constructed in early life and often has to be reconstructed throughout life. Thus, in this framework, cognitive development is being increasingly seen as a *lifelong* process, rather than one which simply starts and ends with childhood (Lerner 1984).

Criticisms of social constructivism again echo those of constructivism in general. Although the ideas briefly illustrated here appear to provide richer accounts of the relation between the individual and the social, they can often seem vague or nebulous. The accounts are perhaps better characterised, in fact, as plausible descriptions or sketches of processes, rather than theory as such. Thus, rarely do we find clear predictions of the consequences of particular perturbations or interventions, which would be a clear indication that we had a good theory. Of course, many would argue that we could hardly expect anything more than such sketches, given the complexity of the phenomena in question. And such arguments are acceptable, so long as we remember that they are largely products of inductive observation that still need to be rigorously tested.

The other criticism is that as social constructivism has emerged it seems to have become increasingly confined to the cognitive domain of human psychology. Affective aspects of the mind have been relatively neglected. So that when social constructivists see the human mind being situated in social activity, rather than encapsulated in the individual head, we do not know to what extent this includes emotions or feelings, or just cognitions. Clearly, emotions and feelings vary from one social situation to the next, and our cognitions and our behaviour seem to be inextricably tied up with them. A comprehensive theory of the relation between mind and society obviously needs to take all of these aspects into account.

References

Ardrey, R. (1969) *The Territorial Imperative*. London, Fontana.

Bandura, A. (1986) *The Social Foundations of Thought and Action*. Englewood Cliffs, Prentice-Hall.

Barash, D. (1979) *The Whispering Within*. Harmondsworth, Penguin.

Beckwith, J. (1987) Criticism and realism. *The Behavioral and Brain Sciences*, 10, 72–3.

Bowlby, J. (1969) *Attachment and Loss*, Vol. 1, *Attachment*. London, Hogarth Press.

Bruner, J. (1964) The course of cognitive growth. *American Psychologist*, 19, 1–15.

Bruner, J.S. (1981) The organisation of action and the nature of adult–infant interaction. In G. d'Ydewalle and W. Lens (eds.), *Cognition in Human Motivation and Learning*. Leuven, Leuven University Press and Lawrence Erlbaum.

Bruner, J.S. (1983) *In Search of Mind*. New York, Harper & Row.

Butterworth, G. and Light, P. (eds.) (1981) *Social Cognition: Studies in the Development of Understanding*. Brighton, Harvester.

Carpenter, F. (1974) *The Skinner Primer*. New York, Free Press.

Doise, W. (1985) On the social development of the intellect. In V.L. Shulman, L.C.R. Restaino-Baumann and L. Butler (eds.), *The Future of Piagetian Theory: The Neo-Piagetians*. New York, Plenum Press

Doise, W. and Mugny, G. (1984) *The Social Development of the Intellect*. London, Academic Press.

Donaldson, M. (1978) *Children's Minds*. London, Fontana.

Dumont, L. (1965) The modern conception of the individual: notes on its genesis and that of concomitant institutions. *Contributions to Indian Sociology*, 8, 13–61.

Eibl-Eibesfeldt, I. (1983) Patterns of parent–child interaction in a cross-cultural perspective. In A. Oliverio and M. Zappella (eds.), *The Behavior of Human Infants*. New York, Plenum Press.

Evans, R.I. (1975) *Konrad Lorenz: The Man and His Ideas*. New York, Harcourt, Brace, Jovanovich.

Geertz, C. (1962) The growth of culture and the evolution of mind. In I.M. Scher (ed.), *Theories of the Mind*. New York, The Free Press of Glenco.

Holloway, R.L. (1975) *The Role of Human Social Behavior in the Evolution of the Brain*. New York, American Museum of Natural History.

Ingleby, D. (1987) Development in social context. In M. Richards and P. Light (eds.), *Children of Social Worlds*. Cambridge, Polity.

Kitcher, P. (1985) *Vaulting Ambition: Sociobiology and the Quest for Human Nature*. Cambridge, Mass., MIT Press.

Kitcher, P. (1987) Precis of *Vaulting ambition: sociobiology and the quest for human nature*. *The Behavioural and Brain Sciences*, 10, 61–100.

Lerner, M. (1984) *On the Nature of Human Plasticity*. Cambridge, Cambridge University Press.

Light, P. (1983) Social interaction and cognitive development: a review of post-Piagetain research. In S. Meadows (ed.), *Developing Thinking*. London, Methuen.

Lorenz, K. (1966) *On Aggression*. London, Methuen.

Lumsden, C.J. and Wilson, E.O. (1981). *Genes, Mind and Culture*. Cambridge, Mass., Harvard University Press.

McDougall, W. (1968) *An Introduction to Social Psychology*. London, Methuen.

McLuhan, M. (1962) *The Guttenburg Galaxy*. London, Routledge and Kegan Paul.

Marx, K. (1973) *Grundrisse*. Harmondsworth, Penguin in association with *New Left Review*.

Mead, G.H. (1937) *Self and Society*. Chicago, University of Chicago Press.

Meltzoff, A.N. and Moore, M.K. (1983) The origins of imitation in infancy: paradigm, phenomena, and theories. In L.P. Lipsitt and C.K. Rovee-Collier (eds.), *Advances in Infancy Research*, Vol. 2. Norwood, New Jersey, Ablex.

Morris, D. (1967) *The Naked Ape*. London, Jonathan Cape.

Perret-Clermont, A-N. (1980) *Social Interaction and Cognitive Development in Children*. London, Academic Press.

Perret-Clermont, A-N. and Bell, N. (1987) Learning processes in social and instructional interactions. In K. Richardson and S. Sheldon (eds.), *Cognitive Development to Adolescence*. Hove, Lawrence Erlbaum.

Piaget, J. (1932) *The Moral Judgement of the Child*. London, Routledge & Kegan Paul.

Pigott, H.E., Fantuzzo, J.W. and Clement, P.W. (1986) The effects of reciprocal peer tutoring and group contingencies on the academic performance of elementary school children. *Journal of Applied Behavior Analysis*, 19, 93–8.

Racklin, H. (1970) *Modern Behaviorism*. San Francisco, W.H. Freeman.

Reykowski, J. (1982) Social motivation. *Annual Review of Psychology*, 33, 23–54.

Richards, M. and Light, P. (1987) *Children of Social Worlds*. Cambridge, Polity.

Russell, B. (1962) *Wisdom of the West*. London, Macdonald.

Skinner, B.F. (1972) *Beyond Freedom and Dignity*. London, Cape.

Strain, P. (ed.) (1981) *The Utilisation of Classroom Peers as Behaviour Change Agents*. New York, Plenum Press.

Tiger, L. and Fox, R. (1971) *The Imperial Animal*. New York, Holt, Rinehart & Winston.

Trevarthen, C. (1983) Interpersonal abilities of infants as generators for transmission of language and culture. In A. Oliverio and M. Zappella (eds.), *The Behavior of Human Infants*, Vol. 2. New York, Plenum Press.

Washburn, S.L. and Howell, F.C. (1960) Human evolution and culture. In S. Tax (ed.), *The Evolution of Man*, Vol. 2. Chicago, University of Chicago Press.

Wertsch, J.V. (ed.) (1981) *The Concept of Activity in Soviet Psychology*. New York, Sharpe.

Whitehead, A.N. (1928) *Science and the Modern World*. Cambridge, Cambridge University Press.

Wilson, O.E. (1975) *Sociobiology: The New Synthesis*. Cambridge, Mass., Harvard University Press.

Wilson, O.E. (1979) *On Human Nature*. Cambridge, Mass., Harvard University Press.

6
Whither Psychology?

If psychology as a discipline is in a bit of a mess at the moment, full of self-doubt about its aims and objectives, fragmented in its activities, disagreeable about what is currently 'good' psychology, whilst always looking for the latest candidate coming up fast on the rails to show us the firmer ground, then there is nothing new about this. Quotes could be produced from writers centuries apart to illustrate the perpetuation of these problems (some such quotes have already been presented in this book). Some have argued that this situation is inevitable in psychology: that there will always be 'a thousand theories blooming'; that there is even virtue in a 'healthy eclecticism' where both professionals and clients can shop around (as in a kind of supermart) for ideas that suit their current needs and feelings; that psychology can never be a true science.

This is not the view taken in this book. Nor do I feel that these are views that the student of psychology should have to become resigned to. Certainly, students need to be quite realistic (and also reassured) about this *being* the current situation in psychology. But instead of the strategies of adaptation usually found among psychology students (including the superficial eclecticism just mentioned), this book makes a plea for a new age of criticism in psychology. It is important that you, *the student*, take up this challenge for many reasons: not least because seasoned academics are already steeped in the going conceptual furniture and probably committed to a particular line. We will turn below to some of the difficulties that need to be overcome. But first let us consider some of the substantive reasons *why* this is a major challenge.

The importance of psychology

When students are asked why they think psychology is important they usually come up with a variety of conclusions like the following:

1. Because it helps us to deal with people better in a wide range of ordinary situations.

2. Because it helps us to treat mental diseases of various kinds.
3. Because it helps us to understand how children develop and therefore to promote development, especially learning in schools.
4. Because it helps us to understand ourselves and thus promote our personal success and happiness in the world.
5. Because it helps us to understand the causes of various kinds of human conflict and thus to try to resolve them.
6. Because it helps us to identify people with certain abilities and potentials, as in occupational and educational selection.
7. Because it helps us to understand how we think, and therefore to build machines that will do our thinking for us (perhaps more efficiently).

This is not intended as an exhaustive list, but it is hopefully representative. The point of this book is not simply to stress that there is considerable fundamental conflict among psychologists about the dealings, treatments, understandings, identifications, and so on, in every one of these statements. Each of them is, indeed, the seed-bed of countless conflicting theories. The point is to stress that, individually or collectively, they *grossly understate* the importance of psychology. Why is this so?

The understatement is due to the fact that psychology is peculiar as a science in that it has repeatedly tried to solve various 'practical' problems without first solving the problem that represents the heart of the discipline. In Chapter 1 we likened this situation to medieval medicine, and went on to explain how 'modern' psychology is still riddled with *ad hoc* theories. We went on further to argue that we have this situation, not simply because psychology has problems with its research methods, or other aspects of practising science – rather it is a problem of a chronic lack of criticism failing to tie these theories down to fundamentals.

The nature of knowledge as the fundamental problem of psychology, of knowledge as the heart of the 'psyche' and therefore of what *defines* psychology as a distinct discipline has been hinted at in every chapter so far. The problem lurks behind every one of the statements above. It has been (apart from the behaviourist doctrines) the acknowledged subject of psychological theory for over two thousand years. This is not to argue that psychologists studying visual perception, cerebral lesions or motor development are not true psychologists. The point is that the research and 'data' of psychologists everywhere can be informed, given direction, evaluated and unified only in the context of a theory of knowledge. In this sense 'knowledge' and 'mind' are virtually synonymous, and to treat any of the statements above without a theory of knowledge is to treat people as mindless.

Just as students adopt simplifying strategies, so do psychologists. Instead of fundamental criticism we get mutual standoffishness in which psychologists flourish in their own 'schools' with their own journals, conferences, and so on, and little cross-talk between them. Instead of facing up to the complexities of the problem, we get retreat into safer havens like biology, neurophysiology, psychophysics, and so on, with the comfortable feeling that this *alone* is somehow making us more scientific. But trying to solve *ad hoc* problems with *ad hoc* theories, or otherwise trying to do 'good things' in psychology, only leads us into longer-term entanglements. When, for instance, Kessen (1962) complains of a 'musty smell' in psychology, it is, as he explains, 'not the smell of dead issues but of issues buried alive' (p. 56). The smell has probably got worse over the last quarter of a century.

The point is that in burying these issues we are burying the real importance of psychology. For without some consensus or majority agreement among psychologists concerning what knowledge *is*, and how it functions, we can never feel really secure about what we know, even in our most secure domains of advanced knowledge like physics and chemistry. And if we have doubts about this, then there must always be doubts about how knowledge – particularly scientific knowledge – is to be created: in sum, what science is and how it should be practised. As Sigmund Koch (1964, p. 5) once put it: 'philosophy and, more generally, the methodology of science are beginning to stand on foundations that only psychology could render secure'.

This is why psychology is a kind of 'superscience', or why it has been called 'the science of sciences': so much depends on it. The age of science has produced wonders; and physics, chemistry and biology have had great days. But now science itself and the advanced disciplines look increasingly to psychology for secure foundations. So psychology has got all its great days ahead, and students with critical minds can look forward to exciting times, quite apart from the practical problems which are deemed to be the major source of psychology's current importance.

These, however, raise other problems. Before considering them further, let us turn again to the strategy adopted in this book for trying to make psychology understandable.

The three theories of knowledge

No psychology – even of the most simplistic 'practical problem-solving' kind – can in fact operate without a theory of knowledge, even if it is a deeply implicit one, and even if it only takes the form of hierarchies or chains of S-R bonds. Sometimes, of course, the theories are rich and highly explicit. But always they relate back to popular conceptions of human nature, which tend to be abstractions fashioned from experience with the behaviour of other people in the real societies in which we and they live and the problems thus created. Sometimes we have formed these abstractions ourselves, perhaps in the form of vague 'hunches'; more usually they have been received in the form of more or less clear tenets from authority figures such as parents, teachers, academics, political leaders, and so on. We accept them to the extent that they help us 'make sense' of our own social experience and make it more predictable. Because they involve tenets about how people think, feel and act (in other words 'know'), such abstractions have formed the basis of phychological theories of knowledge (and thereby more general theories in psychology) for centuries. And because they are not *originally* scientific facts, but popular conceptions, we have called them, in this book, *presuppositions*. Finally, it has been argued in this book that the contemporary range of psychological theories can be connected with three distinct sets of presuppositions, elaborated by psychologists and now widely recognised as rationalism or nativism, associationism or empiricism, and constructivism. Each set implies a pre-scientific theory of 'knowing', and therefore a theory of human nature.

Of course, in having a genetic connection with pre-scientific conceptions of reality, psychological theories are no different from those in any other science. The myth of pure science, somehow operating in isolation from the ordinary experience of people, has long been exploded. In Chapter 1 we cited scientists and philosophers of science, from Einstein through Collingwood to the more recent challengers like Feyerabend, to the effect that every theory arises from a question, but every question is based on a presupposition.

The difference in psychology is that it is extremely difficult to 'objectify' ourselves from the presuppositions arising from common experience. This is simply because psychologists themselves almost invariably act in, and work for, a particular social situation which largely determines their own experience of other people, including the questions about them that they try to answer. In the other sciences there has at least been some progress in this respect, though often only by determined struggle in the face of prejudice. Among the best authorities, as in popular experience, the earth was once the centre of the universe; disease was the result of some evil; and evolution the result of blind competition within and between populations. In all of these respects science has changed (or at least is changing) the popular preconceptions. But in psychology this has not happened; our theories of knowing are still closely connected with such popular preconceptions.

There is nothing new about these points, and the genetic connections are not difficult to see. Wherever societies are organised in the form of rigid and stratified divisions of labour, wealth and power, rationalism or nativisim arises naturally as a way of helping us 'make sense' of this social experience. Wherever we need people (or animals) to be rapidly trained and retrained for fairly docile roles, associationism will do and, indeed, did for generations of animal trainers, long before psychologists introduced it to the human domain. Wherever the popular need is felt for fundamental social transformation, and creative reconstruction, constructivism arises as a popular conception of human nature; hence Kant's theory of knowledge paralleled revolutionary ferments in the late eighteenth century, and developments of it inspired those of the early nineteenth century.

So psychology is fragmented and bewildering to the psychology student, because its kaleidoscopic theories are based on a multiplicity of theories of, or presuppositions about, knowledge. Why this multiplicity? Because there is a social need for it.

To understand this let us reflect again on how presuppositions enter into our theories. It may be helpful for you to glance again at Figure 1.2 (p. 9) for this. Here we see how presuppositions arise as abstractions from common experience. But to the scientist they are primitive theories which guide initial observation. In any case, when we start theorising scientifically, we make systematic observations in order to identify the *components* of the system being considered, and also their properties. In order to make the system 'come alive', however, a good theory must also describe the *relations* between these components (see Figure 1.1, p. 5). Presuppositions are brought in here to make the system 'work'. Among the many examples given so far are Chomsky's innate structures, Thorndike's S-R bonds and Piaget's dynamics of construction.

The objective of the hypothetico-deductive phase of research is then to put the theory to the test to see if it really does work in the way posited. In this way our presuppositions may become reinforced. A point we shall have to make subsequently is that we can be exceptionally naïve and simplistic about these testings and reinforcings. But the point we have to make immediately is the obvious one that, if psychology is to be unified like the other sciences, it cannot have such conflicting presuppositions coexisting; some (or all) will have to be dropped. But shedding them as the result of criticism, or supplanting them as the result of research, can be an extremely painful business, because it means detaching ourselves from our view of experience and moving to another one.

Goldstein and Goldstein (1978, p. 274) illustrate this with the problem of thinking of the world as round instead of flat:

> To make such a leap in thought, it was necessary to overcome one basic concept we all have developed from our earliest experiences: the concept of *up* and *down*. It is easy for us, having been indoctrinated with the idea, both in school and out of it . . . to be aware that up and down in China or Australia are different from up and down in New York or London. But a young child . . . takes as given the idea that *down* is the unique direction in which things fall and *up* is its opposite. The basic experiences that define these directions do not hint to us that they are relative. One can see what a leap of the imagination, what a denial of the obvious and unquestioned, was involved in thinking of a round earth.

In Chapter 1 we mentioned the switch from a geocentric to a heliocentric view of the universe as another example. In nearly every case progress towards unified science has depended on the overthrow of what at first seemed most obvious. But (as we shall also discuss later) this involves a *critical* as well as an empirical process. As Goldstein and Goldstein (1978, p. 274) say about such discoveries: 'all of them do involve to some extent a process of making explicit what had previously been tacitly accepted, and challenging it'.

Note that, whilst it is correct to point to a rough correspondence between psychological theory, its presuppositions and social need, the connection is not a simple or direct one. We must not argue that the *producers* of theories are themselves culpable, conscious or unconscious bearers of ideology because of what their theories invariably presuppose. The point is that ultimately theorising becomes dogged by those presuppositions because that is what largely determines its *acceptability* as psychological theory.

Thus, Chomsky's theory of predetermined language structures and structures of the mind does not mean that Chomsky is ideologising for a rigid, hierarchic state. On the contrary, he sees his theory as having liberating implications, rather than repressive ones (see Chomsky 1968). But it is the fate of the theory that is the important point. Chomsky's original theory was enthusiastically accepted within linguistics strictly for its scientific credentials (its theoretical rigour, clarity in describing components of language, their properties and relations, and so on; and, therefore, the ease with which it generated testable predictions or hypotheses). Innate structures were incorporated as the 'glue' of the theory because Chomsky – like Descartes and Plato before him – simply could not see any alternative.

The extension of the theory into psychology, however, was accepted for two reasons. First, because it served as a shining model of theorising about *internal* processes, at a time when behaviourism was being attacked for its ineffectiveness. Second, because the idea of innate structures, which could easily be computer-programs-in-the-head, chimed in well with the information-processing approach that was growing at the time. As time went on, however, the rationalist aspects of the theory became increasingly important (see Chapter 2), so that today we have the ironic situation in which Chomsky's innate structures have a significant place in psychology, whereas his linguistic theory, by his own admission, is now shared by only a 'tiny minority' in linguistics (see the interesting discussion with Chomsky in Gardner 1985). The reason for this may be that, as Shotter (1987) put it, the artificial intelligence movement is predicated on people 'working in terms of hierarchies of domination along mechanical lines' (p. 49), and that cognitivism *augments* behaviourism rather than supplants it (Reed 1987).

So we are not arguing that the incorporation of presuppositions into theory is a direct and conscious attempt to subserve social needs in the way the original presuppositions do – only that the *fate* of theories is, to some extent, determined by the needs. Nor are we arguing that individual psychologists or individual theories are necessary *either-or* rationalist, associationist or constructivist.

For instance, specific theories may be 'mixed', in the sense that they try to import two, or all three, sets of presuppositions in different measure. Thus, it has been proposed that a child is born with quite *well-formed* mental operations, which undergo steady maturation, but which, at the same time, give rise to further mental constructions – i.e. a rationalist augmentation of Piaget's constructivism (Mounoud and Vinter 1985). Since Anderson and Bower (1973), much cognitive theory has been based on the idea of a knowledge store (or memory) based on associations, put there and operated upon by innate mental processes (i.e. a mixture of rationalism and associationism). Some theories of 'general intelligence' seem to view intelligence as a system, partly of learning by associations, and partly of learning by abstractions, or constructions; yet at the same hypothesise that the global capacity is quite innately well formed, because individual *differences* in it are said to be largely innate (Jensen 1973). As we mentioned in Chapter 2, a number of theories envisage some quite tight 'constraints' on what is, or is not, learned (which learning may take place by associationist or constructivist means).

Some people see nothing wrong in – or indeed openly encourage – theories in which 'this' may be innate, while 'that' may develop constructively, and 'the other' will learn by associations. This view seems to arise out of the attempt to find a compromise, or line of least resistance, rather than a genuine solution to the problem. But it leaves us with a rather messy, fragmented mind, which is difficult to entertain without a clear, positive rationale for doing so. The mind is, we must presume, a unified system, and therefore deserves a unified theory, not one which says that the system is partly pre-programmed, partly constructs programmes and partly registers associations, according to our tastes of the moment. So such compromises need to be very critically examined.

Another common form of compromise is what might be called 'interactionism'. A proponent of this view would simply argue that *all* characters are partly determined innately, and partly by environment and experience, with the final product being determined by interaction between genes and environment in the course of development. Such a view appears to get us off the twin hooks of the nature–nurture debate, but only by lumping together all polygenic characters (somatic, physiological, behavioural, psychological) as of one and the same type. But greater discretion than this is required. Different characters have different evolutionary histories, connected with peculiar selection pressures and their peculiar functions. Thus, adaptation in a fairly constant environment might entail selection for characters that are strongly resistant to variability of expression in the course of development (i.e. little if any interaction). A somewhat changeable or 'patchy' environment might demand variable genetic expression with considerable gene–environment interaction. An *extremely* changeable and variable environment might demand a different strategy: non-variable genetic expression to the point of a phenotype that constantly reshapes *itself* by interacting very closely with the environment (Plotkin and Odling-Smee 1979). The mammalian immune system is one example of this latter strategy; the human language and human mental systems may be others. But whatever the particular case, complex characters are under the control of finely integrated gene *systems* that are common to all members of a species, and are transmitted as such from parents to offspring (Mayr 1970). It is not true to say, as does Gleitman (1986, p. 455), that 'Each sperm cell of a given male is produced by a kind of genetic lottery . . . Similarly for the female's egg cell.' Such an anarchic view only reflects more starkly the need for coherent psychological theory.

The role of criticism

Can psychology, then, ever be a detached science? Or is it doomed to playing the role of fragmented semi-science and supplier of ideological 'in-fill'? As argued in Chapter 1, sciences progress to the extent that they ascend to positions of relative detachment from popular preconceptions of nature. The term 'relative' is important: physics, chemistry and biology are far from being completely free of social determination in the shaping of their theories. But these have at least constructed theories that are *relatively* detached from common experience, and the most important indication of this is that a large majority of scientists agree with them. These achievements have been wrought by persistent criticism and conceptual purification.

Although the 'scientific revolution' of the seventeenth century is usually attributed to the installation of empirical methods, the habit of *conceptual* testing and scrutiny was at least equally important. For instance, although Galileo's triumph over the Aristotelian conservatives of the age is usually attributed to his experimental methods, as Hall (1963, pp. 75–6) pointed out:

> only rarely did Galileo claim that the Aristotelians erred in their facts because they had not experimented to discover them. Rather, it was their failure to consider facts correctly that he constantly stressed. His chief target was the absurdity of their reasoning . . . It was an intellectual revolution that Galileo effected.

The intellectual revolution consisted precisely of the effort and freedom to criticise, and this (assisted, of course, by empirical methods) is precisely what led to rapid developments in the advanced sciences. And it is a process which continues to this day. Witness, for example, the numerous contemporary critiques of Darwinism and the currently accepted evolutionary synthesis (see e.g. Gould 1982; Eldredge 1985).

Goldstein and Goldstein (1978) illustrate this point further with the subject of heat, and the conflict between the caloric and kinetic theories of heat in the eighteenth and nineteenth centuries. As they first point out: 'The scientific study of heat, like much else in science, has its roots in the most primitive experiences of daily life' (p. 63). Popular intuition and early scientific theory of heat conceived of heat as a substance. The question became particularly prominent in the eighteenth century because of the increasing practical problems involving heat, created by the Industrial Revolution, and the idea that heat was a substance (caloric) was restated in a slightly more elaborate form. As these authors point out, although the theory turned out to be wrong, 'none the less a number of significant properties of heat were discovered with its help' (p. 65) and 'at that time it explained much of the then known properties of heat' (p. 66). A rival theory, called the kinetic theory, was based on the idea of heat as high frequency vibrations, either in the substance of a body or in its atoms.

The next development was the introduction of major *conceptual* distinctions between temperature and heat, and also the heat *capacities* of different materials – all of which generated a number of hypotheses which led to results supporting the caloric theory. But supporters of the kinetic theory – in particular Count Rumford – questioned the reasoning in these predictions and conclusions, and sought more critical predictions which would discriminate between the two theories. They reasoned, for instance, that if heat is a substance, objects should weigh less as they cool down. But in experiments this did not happen. Thus, for a time, one theory seemed to account better for one set of facts, the other for another set of facts. But the critical reasoning went on. As Goldstein and Goldstein (1978, p. 103) note: 'It took 50 years from the time of Rumford's experiments for the kinetic theory to develop to the point where it could explain those phenomena that the caloric theory explained so well.'

What this illustrates is how critical attacks on presuppositions have the effect of 'opening up' the closed explanatory system that particular theories serve. In psychology, at present, almost any set of observations that is the subject of a psychological theoretical construction, based on one set of presuppositions, nearly always gives rise, just as happily, to alternative theoretical constructions based on rival presuppositions. It then becomes a fairly simple matter to 'confirm' any one of these in an experiment. This happens all the time in psychology. What very rarely happens is experiments done which simultaneously eliminate rival theories. Yet this is what must be demanded, and what criticism of presuppositions will help bring. As increasing numbers of students develop these habits, these responsibilities will be increasingly brought home to journal editors, referees and other commentators, too. The fruits of this general movement will almost certainly be conceptual clarification and greater objectivity in psychology, which in turn will mean more *general* theory of humanity, freed from a *particular* social time and social place but, by virtue of that, more applicable to all.

A critical psychology?

It is too early to tell whether psychology will ever harness superb methodology to critical reasoning, and thus achieve theoretical resolution in this way. In his recent history of psychology, Hearnshaw (1987, pp. 298–9) notes that there have been enormous swings of fashion in the last few decades: 'But unification is still but a dream.' One of his dreams is of 'a comprehensive overview of psychology, embracing all aspects of the subject. It is such a synoptic view that psychology urgently requires to reconcile its differences and discipline its vagaries.' I would hope that this book will help make such an achievement more possible.

References

Anderson, J.R. and Bower, G.H. (1973) *Human Associative Memory*. New York, Wiley.
Chomsky, N. (1968) *Language and Mind*. New York, Harcourt, Brace & World.
Eldredge, N. (1985) *Unfinished Synthesis: Biological Hierarchies and Modern Evolutionary Thought*. Oxford, Oxford University Press.
Gardner, H. (1985) *The Mind's New Science*. New York, Basic Books.
Gleitman, H. (1986) *Psychology*. New York, Norton.
Goldstein, M. and Goldstein, I.F. (1978) *How We Know: An Exploration of the Scientific Process*. New York, Plenum Press.
Gould, S.J. (1982) Darwinism and the expansion of evolutionary theory. *Science*, 216, 380–7.
Hall, A.R. (1963) *From Galileo to Newton, 1630–1720*. London, Collins.
Hearnshaw, L.S. (1987) *The Shaping of Modern Psychology*. London, Routledge & Kegan Paul.
Jensen, A.R. (1973) *Educability and Group Differences*. London, Methuen.
Kessen, W. (1962) 'Stage' and 'structure' in the study of children. *Monographs of the Society for Research in Child Development*, 27, 65–86.
Koch, S. (1964) Psychology and the emerging conceptions of knowledge as unitary. in T. Mann (ed.), *Behaviorism and Phenomenology*. Chicago, University of Chicago Press.
Mayr, E. (1970) *Populations, Species and Evolution*. Cambridge, Mass., Belknap Press of Harvard University Press.
Mounoud, P. and Vinter, A. (1985) A theoretical developmental model: the self-image in children. In V.L. Shulman, L.C.R. Restaino-Bauman and L. Butler (eds.), *The Future of Piagetian Theory: The Neo-Piagetians*. New York, Plenum Press.

Plotkin, H.C. and Odling-Smee, F.J. (1979) Learning, change and evolution: an enquiry into the teleonomy of learning. *Advances in the Study of Behavior*, 10, 1–42.

Reed, S. (1987) Why do things look as they do: the implications of James Gibson's 'The Ecological Approach to Visual Perception'. In A. Costall and A. Still (eds.), *Cognitive Psychology in Question*. New York, St Martin's Press.

Shotter, J. (1987) Cognitive Psychology, Taylorism and the manufacture of unemployment. In A. Costall and A. Still (eds.), *Cognitive Psychology in Question*. New York, St Martin's Press.

Index